THE RISE OF MODERN RELIGIOUS IDEAS IN AMERICA

– Editorial Director –

SYDNEY E. AHLSTROM, American Studies Program, Yale University

BORDEN P. BOWNE

Philosophy of Theism

Reprint Edition
with a New Introduction

THE REGINA PRESS

Reprint Edition 1975

THE REGINA PRESS
7 Midland Avenue
Hicksville, New York 11801

New Introduction © 1975 by The Regina Press

Library of Congress Catalog Number: 74-78274
International Standard Book Number: 0-88271-012-5

This volume is reprinted according to the standards established in 1972 by the Rare Book Libraries' Conference on Facsimiles.

Manufactured in the United States of America.

THE PERSONALISM of Borden Parker Bowne, writes W. H. Werkmeister in his *History of Philosophical Ideas In America*, was "the first complete and comprehensive system of philosophy developed in America which has had lasting influence and which still counts some of our outstanding thinkers among its adherents." Herbert W. Schneider, in his *History of American Philosophy*, makes a similar judgement, declaring that Bowne "was one of the most gifted teachers and independent minds of his generation." One could go even farther and venture the proposition that no American philosopher has ever equalled Bowne's hold on a large academic discipleship or attained so large an influence on the religious thinking of so large a lay constituency. His influence was largely due to the commanding position of his thought in the seminaries, colleges, and universities affiliated with the Methodist Church, which up to the time of his death was the largest Protestant denomination in the United States. Despite the importance of the far flung educational system of a very well organized denomination, however, Bowne was anything but an autocrat. At one point he was even threatened by a heresy trial. Basically his influence stemmed from his effectiveness as a teacher, his gift for lively and persuasive exposition, and his capacity to develop a coherent theistic doctrine of personalism at a time when post-Darwinian thought and naturalistic positivism were threatening the moral and religious composure of many Americans.

Borden Parker Bowne (1847-1910) was born in Leonardsville, New Jersey and received his undergraduate education at New York University at a time when it was more a self-consciously Methodist institution than it later became. The decisive turn in his philosophic career took place during his post-graduate studies in Germany between 1871 and 1873. In the exciting intellectual life of the Universities of Halle and Gottingen, he like so many other American scholars, philosophers, and theologians, found his entire outlook transformed. Most immediately it was the seriousness, thoroughness, and intellectual boldness of German thought and scholarship that impressed these visiting Americans. Yet in the long run it was the intellectual substance that became most important, and for Bowne this came chiefly from two great professors. By J. E. Erdmann he was introduced to the history of philosophy, which ever since Hegel has become a creative and enlivening education force. From Rudolf Hermann Lotze (1817-1881) his thought was given the direction that it maintained to the end. Indeed, in his *Metaphysics, A Study fo First Principles* (1882) Bowne concedes that "the conclusions reached are those of Lotze." In making this confession, incidentally, Bowne was far more candid than the many others of his generation, down even to George Santayana, who owed much to Lotze's lifelong effort to reconstruct an idealistic system of thought that would at the same time be fully compatible with modern science and the concept of mechanism in nature.

In 1876, after a period of journalistic activity, Bowne was called to Boston University where he served as a professor of philosophy until his death. It is important to recognize, moreover, that he understood his role as primarily philosophical, not theological, even though it might be said that a rational legitimation of theism was his life's chief objective. In chapter V of the present work, for example, the question of miracles is discussed in abstract terms with no reference to the stormy controversies on this subject that were agitating the churches. This does not mean, on the other hand, that Bowne's influence on American theology was negligible. His disciple at Boston University, A. C. Knudson (1873-1953) expounded a personalist theology in many volumes. In addition to writing an excellent biography, Francis J. McConnell (1871-1953), Methodist bishop and influential social actionist, also translated Bowne's ideas into theory and practice. Still later Edgar S. Brightman extended Bowne's influence far into the twentieth century. One sees distinctive marks of Bowne's outlook even in the thought of Martin Luther King, who received his PhD from Boston University in 1958. Because of its idealistic emphasis on the self as the basis and presupposition of all judgements about the world, as well as its accent on human freedom, personalist theology has with justice been referred to as Neo-Arminian.

Bowne's works cover the whole realm of philosophical concern, from his first work, *Studies in Theism* (1879) which was revised and updated in the volume at hand (1898), on through his *Metaphysics* (1882); *Introduction to Psychological Theory* (1886); *The Principles of Ethics* (1892); *The Theory of Thought and Knowledge* (1897); *Christian Revelation* (1898); *The Immanence of God* (1905); *Personalism* (1908) and two posthumous volumes: *The Essence of Religion* (1910) and *Kant and Spencer, A Critical Exposition* (1912). In this last named work he returns to one of the earliest and most continuous concerns of his life's work.

Bowne was convinced that the primary intellectual and religious need of his times, for mankind in general or Christianity in particular, was an alternative to naturalistic impersonalism. Atheistic mechanism was unsatisfactory because it reduces thought and belief to mental events, "one is good as another while it lasts . . . . No system of necessity has any standard of distinction between truth and error." (pp.113,114). Theism, on the contrary is a belief that can deal with problems of purpose teleology, ethics, and thought. It thus provides the only satisfactory account of the whole of reality.

No conviction was more central to Bowne's system than this theistic argument. Yet his position was modestly taken. Theism may be "the sum and source" of ideas that rule our life, yet he granted that this view like our entire mental life rests upon a fallacy, on an "illicit process": our conclusions are too large for the premises. "In short, while theism is demonstrated by nothing, it is implicit in everything."

Bibliographical Suggestions:

A. C. Knudson, *The Philosophy of Personalism* (1927); Francis J. Mc Connell, *Borden Parker Bowne* (1929); Edgar S. Brightman, "Personalism and The Influence of Bowne" *Proceedings of The Sixth International Congress of Philosophy,* E. S. Brightman, ed. (New York: Longmans, Green and Company, 1927).

PHILOSOPHY OF THEISM

BY

BORDEN P. BOWNE

PROFESSOR OF PHILOSOPHY IN BOSTON UNIVERSITY

AUTHOR OF "METAPHYSICS" "INTRODUCTION TO
PSYCHOLOGICAL THEORY" ETC.

NEW YORK

HARPER & BROTHERS, FRANKLIN SQUARE

CONTENTS.

CHAPTER   PAGE

      INTRODUCTION 1

  I. UNITY OF THE WORLD-GROUND. 41

 II. THE WORLD-GROUND AS INTELLIGENT 62

III. THE WORLD-GROUND AS PERSONAL 122

IV. THE METAPHYSICAL ATTRIBUTES OF THE WORLD-GROUND 139

  V. GOD AND THE WORLD 171

 VI. THE WORLD-GROUND AS ETHICAL 211

VII. THEISM AND LIFE 241

    CONCLUSION 261

PREFACE.

THIS work does not aim to say everything about theism. I have rather sought to give an outline of the essential argument which might serve as a text for teachers and as a somewhat critical survey of the subject for other readers.

Kant pointed out that the ontological argument properly proves nothing, and that the cosmological and the design argument depend on the ontological. The argument, then, is not demonstrative, and rests finally on the assumed existence of a perfect being. In a different form I have maintained the same position; but so far from concluding that theistic faith is baseless, I have sought to show that essentially the same postulate underlies our entire mental life. There is an element of faith and volition latent in all our theorizing. Where we cannot prove, we believe. Where we cannot demonstrate, we choose sides. This element of faith cannot be escaped in any field of thought, and without it the mind is helpless and dumb. Oversight of this fact has led to boundless verbal haggling and barren logic-chopping, in which it would be hard to say whether the affirmative or the negative be the more confused. Absurd demands for " proof" have been met with absurd " proofs." The argument has thus been transferred from the field of life and action, where it mainly belongs, to the arid wastes of formal logic, where it has fared scarcely better than the man who journeyed to Jericho from Jerusalem. The conclusion is that theism is the fundamental postulate of our total life. It cannot, indeed, be demonstrated without assumption, but it cannot be denied without wrecking all our interests.

This claim has been especially emphasized in considering the bearing of theism upon the problem of knowledge. I have sought to show that our cognitive and speculative interests, as well as our moral and religious interests, are so bound up with theism as to stand or fall with it. If we say, then, that theism is strictly proved by nothing, we must also admit that it is implicit in everything. Anti-theistic schemes are generally

in the instinctive stage of thought, where knowledge constitutes no problem and is taken for
granted. In this stage any theory whatever
may be held, however self-destructive; and
when its suicidal implications are pointed out,
the theorist falls back on unreasoned common-
sense, and repudiates, not his own theory, which
is the real offender, but the critic. He sets up
natural selection as the determining principle of
belief, and then repudiates the great catholic
convictions of the race. He shows how the survival of the fittest must bring thought and thing
into accord, and then rejects the beliefs which
survive. He defines mind as an adjustment of
inner relations to outer relations, and forthwith
drifts off into nescience. He presents the Unknown Cause as the source of all beliefs, and
then rules out most of them as invalid, and, at
times, declares them all worthless. This pitia-
ble compound of instinct and reflection, in which
each destroys the other, has even been regarded
as the final philosophy. Such performances are
both saddening and wearisome. It seems clear
that whoever will reason should regard the conditions of reason, and should not set up theories
which undermine reason. But it will be a long

step in advance when this simple principle is recognized. Meanwhile the critic must possess his tired soul in patience when he sees suicidal theories parading as science and supreme wisdom. The greater the dearth of thought, the greater the swarm of opinions.

Yet there is some progress. Except in philosophy and theology, there is coming to be a decided conviction that no one has a right to an opinion who has not studied the subject. Off-hand decisions of unstudied questions receive very little consideration nowadays in the sciences. It is to be hoped that this mental seriousness may yet extend to philosophy and theology. At present it is not so. He would be a rare man indeed who could not settle questions in theology or Biblical criticism without previous study; while the small men who could dispose of philosophy and philosophers in one afternoon are legion. Meanwhile the irrelevance, the misunderstanding, the superficiality are so apparent that the student is unavoidably reminded of our first parents, of whom it is said, They were naked and were not ashamed.

That nature when driven out with a fork always comes running back is a discovery of

ancient date. We have an excellent illustration
of this law in the way in which language has
avenged the attempt to discredit the teleological
view of nature. Teleology has taken entire
possession of the language of botany and biology, especially when expounded in terms of
evolution. Even plants do the most acute and
far-sighted things to maintain their existence.
They specialize themselves with a view to cross-
fertilization and make nothing of changing spe-
cies or genus to reach their ends. A supply is
often regarded as fully explained when the need
is pointed out; and evolution itself is not infre-
quently endowed with mental attributes. Such
extraordinary mythology arises from the mental
necessity for recognizing purpose in the world;
and as it would not be good form to speak of a
divine purpose, there is no shift but to attribute
it to "Nature" or "Evolution" or " Law " or some
other of the homemade divinities of the day.

The atheistic gust of recent years has about
blown over. Atheism is dead as a philosophy,
and remains chiefly as a disposition. But the
origin and history of the late atheistic renascence are not without both interest and instruc-
tion. The crude popular realism, joined with

the notion of necessity, furnished excellent soil
for an atheistic growth.   Not a few atheists
found a disproof of theism in the conservation
of energy, and not a few theists felt that all
depended on discrediting that doctrine.   Both
parties alike agreed in the principle, the more
law, the less God.   This grotesque inversion
of reason, together with the doctrine of evolution in biology, brought about a state of triumph on the one side and of panic on the other
which is unintelligible now except to one versed
in the philosophy of error, and which is seen to
be equally baseless in both cases.   The naïve
disportings of the speculators of that period are
at once as charming and as embarrassing to the
modest critic as the contemplation of a state of
paradisaical innocence.   Happily, there is an advance towards clothing and a right mind.   That
terrible necessity which left no room for God
has been recognized as only a shadow of the
mind's own throwing.   Even evolution, that
monster of hideous mien, on the one hand, has
been discovered not to be so potent a solvent
of philosophical questions as was once fancied,
and on the other, even some theists have plucked
up courage enough, not only to endure, but also

to embrace. Fundamental problems are seen to remain about what they always were in spite of the advent of the " New Philosophy." When that philosophy first appeared in the wilderness of the old philosophy and theology, announcing that the kingdom of science was at hand, high hopes were entertained by some, and gloomy forebodings by others, as to what the end would be. But as the attraction of novelty and denial wore off, it became clear that the "New Philosophy" could not hit it off with criticism any more happily than the old. To the apostles, this was both a revelation and a sore disappointment. They meant well and were gifted writers, but they were lacking in patient reflection. They took more heed to their speculative ways and became less enthusiastic but wiser men. Some proof of this is found in the fact that the British Association for the Advancement of Science has not favored us with a cosmological manifesto for the last dozen years. All parties have learned wisdom. Theists have gained breadth and courage. Anti-theists have found that the way of anti-theism is hard. The critic must allow that the theistic outlook was never more encouraging. The only exception to this general

growth is in the case of the newspaper and mag-
azine scientist—that well of omniscience unde-
filed.   Here, as ever, one finds chiefly words and
hearsay, an *exploitation* of what the writer does
not know.   BORDEN P. BOWNE.

BOSTON, *July*, 1887.

PHILOSOPHY OF THEISM.

INTRODUCTION.

§ 1. MAN is religious. However it came about, our race, at least as soon as it emerged from brutishness, possessed religious ideas and impulses. The earth is full of religion; and life and thought, art and literature, are moulded by it.

Concerning this fact three questions may be asked. These concern respectively, (1) the source of religion, (2) the genesis and history of religion, and (3) the rational foundation or warrant of religion.

The Source of Religion.

§ 2. To this question various answers are given. Some have been content to view religion as a device of state and priest craft; but this view has

long been obsolete.   The impossibility of impos-
ing purely adventitious and fictitious ideas upon
the mind by external authority makes it necessary to look for the source of religion within the
mind itself.   Such source was found at a very
early date in fear.   Man being timid and helpless, feigns gods partly to help himself and partly as projections of his fears.   This view, which
finds full expression by Lucretius, has been extended by Hume, who finds the source of religious ideas in the personifying tendency of the
mind.   Man projects his own life into all his objects, and thus surrounds himself with a world of
invisible beings.   Others have held that the idea
of an invisible world first got afloat through
dreams, trances, fits, etc., and once afloat, it took
possession of the human mind in general, with
the exception always of a few choice spirits of
rare insight; and from this unseemly origin the
whole system of religious thought has been
developed.   Suggestions of this kind are numberless.   They are mainly an extension of the
sensational philosophy into the realm of ,re-
ligion.   As that philosophy seeks to reduce the
rational factors of intellect to sensation, and ethical elements to non-ethical, so also it seeks to

reduce the religious nature to something non-religious. But in all of these attempts it succeeds only by tacitly begging the question. If we take a mind whose full nature is expressed in the quality A, it will be forever impossible to develop anything but A out of it. In order to move at all A must be more than A; it must be $A + X$, or XA. That X contains the ground of the movement. A being whose nature is exhausted in sense objects can never transcend them. Everything must be to him what it seems. The stick must be a stick, not a fetich. The sun and moon must be lighted disks and not gods. To get such a being beyond the sense object to a religious object we must endow him with more than the A of sensation, or the B of animal fear. The cattle have both; but only some very hopeful evolutionists have discovered any traces of religion among them; and if it should turn out that these traces are not misleading, it would not prove that simple sensations can become religious ideas, but that the animal mind is more and better than we have been accustomed to think.

Another view has been suggested, that religious ideas are the product of reflective thought. This

view is disproved by experience. Man was religious before he became a philosopher. Speculative thought has had the function of criticis-
ing and clarifying religious ideas, but never of
originating them; and often they have been
much more confidently held without its aid than
with it. On this account many have viewed
speculation in its religious efforts as a kind of
inverted Jacob's ladder.

Hence many have held that religious ideas are
innate. This could only mean that the human
mind is such as to develop religious sentiments
and ideas under the stimulus of our total experience; and experience shows such difference of
religious thought that the content of this religious intuition could hardly be more than a
vague apprehension of an invisible and supernatural existence. The phrase, innate ideas, has
so many misleading connotations that it had
better be avoided.

In the same line it has been suggested that
the soul has a special organ or faculty for the reception of religious truth; and the state of this
faculty has even been made a ground for important theological distinctions. Sometimes it has
been called faith, sometimes feeling, and some-

times the "God-consciousness." But psychology long ago discovered that nothing is explained by reference to a faculty; since the faculty itself is always and only an abstraction from the facts for whose explanation it is invoked or invented. There is probably no question more utterly arid and barren than the search for the "faculty" from which religion springs.

The conclusion is this: No external action can develop an empty mind which has no law, nature, or direction into anything. This would be to act upon the void. Hence it is hopeless to look for the source of religious ideas in external experience alone. We must assume a germ of religious impulse in the soul in order to make religious development possible. But, on the other hand, this germ is not self-sufficient. It develops only under the stimulus of outer and inner experience, and unless under the criticism and restraint of intellect and conscience it develops into grotesque or terrible forms. The stimulus may be manifold. It may lie in our sense of dependence, in the needs of the intellect, in the demands and forebodings of conscience, in the cravings of the affections, in the words of revelation, and in some direct influence of God upon the soul. Which of these it may be, or whether all of them enter into actual religious development, is a question for separate study.

The History of Religion.

§ 3. This question does not concern us. It is referred to (1) because it is a separate question, and (2) because there is a fancy that the truth of religion can be determined by studying its development either in the individual or in the history of the race. But a little reflection shows that the psychological genesis of an idea is not to be confounded with its philosophical worth. When the latter question is up the former is entirely irrelevant, unless it be shown that philosophical value is compatible with only one form of psychological genesis. This showing has never been attempted. Meanwhile the rational value of a proposition can be determined only by considering its content and the reasons which are offered for it.

The Grounds of Religion.

§ 4. But our present concern is with neither of the first two questions, but rather with the third, the rational foundation of religion, and more particularly with the rational foundation of the theistic idea, which is the central conception of religion. We set aside, therefore, all inquiry into the origin and development of religious ideas, and inquire rather whether they have any rational warrant now that they are here. We take, then, what we may call the theistic consciousness of the race as the text for a critical exegesis with the aim of fixing its content and philosophical worth. We do not aim at a philosophical deduction or speculative construction of religion, nor yet at a genetic unfolding of religion; we aim only to analyze and understand the data of the religious consciousness.

The outcome of this inquiry might conceivably be threefold. The theistic idea might be found to be (1) contradictory or absurd, (2) an implication of the religious sentiment only, and without any significance for pure intellect, and (3) a demand of our entire nature, intellectual, moral, æsthetic, and religious. In the first case it would have to be abandoned. In the second it would be a fact of which no further account could be given, but which need not, on that account, be rejected. In the last case theism would appear as the implication of all our faculties, and would have the warrant of the entire soul. How this may be the course of our study must show.

§ 5. The function of the theistic idea in human thought as a whole is very complex. First, theism may be advanced as an hypothesis for the explanation of phenomena. As such it has no religious function at all, but solely a logical and metaphysical one. The question is considered under the law of the sufficient reason; and the aim is to find an adequate explanation of phenomena, especially those of the external world. Most theistic argument has been carried on on this basis. The facts of the outer world have been appealed to, especially those which show adaptation and adjustment to ends; and the claim has been set up that only intelligence could account for them. These facts have been supplemented with various metaphysical considerations concerning the absolute and the relative, the infinite and the finite, the necessary and the contingent, the self-moving and the moved; and the work was done. How far this comes from satisfying the religious nature is evident.

Second, theism may be held as the implication and satisfaction of our entire nature, intellectual,

emotional, æsthetic, ethical, and religious. These
elements reach out after God so naturally and,
when developed, almost so necessarily, that they
have always constituted the chief actual grounds
of theistic belief. Accordingly the human mind
has always adjusted its conception of God with
reference less to external nature than to its own
internal needs and aspirations. It has gathered
its ideals of truth and beauty and goodness, and
united them into the thought of the one Perfect Being, the ideal of ideals, God over all and
blessed forever. A purely ætiological contemplation of the world and life with the sole aim of finding an adequate cause according to the law of the
sufficient reason would give us an altogether different idea of God from that which we possess.

Hence it has been a frequent claim, even among
theologians, that arguments for theism are worthless. They may produce some assent but no
living conviction; and when they are strictly
logical they reach only barren results which
are religiously worthless. These sterilities are
transformed into fruitfulness only by implicitly
falling back on the living religious consciousness; and this might as well be done openly and
at the start.

This claim is partly true and partly false. It is true that purely ætiological arguments, like that from design, are inadequate, but they may be good as far as they go. It is also true that purely metaphysical arguments concerning the absolute, or unconditioned, do not bring us in sight of living religious sentiment, but they have their value nevertheless. On the other hand, it is a grave oversight to suppose that such considerations alone can give the full religious conception of God. The actual grounds of theistic belief are manifold, being intellectual, emotional, æsthetic, and ethical; and no one can understand the history of the belief without taking all of these into account.

But here the very grave doubt meets us whether most of these elements are proper grounds of belief, and whether theistic argument does not confessedly proceed by a much looser logic than obtains in our mental procedure elsewhere. This compels us to take a short survey of mental method in general.

§ 6. It is a traditional superstition of intellect that nothing is to be accepted which is not either self-evident or demonstrated. The corresponding conception of method is this: Let us first find some invincible fact or principle, something which cannot be doubted or denied without absurdity, and from this let us deduce by cogent logic whatever may be got out of it. When we reach the end of our logic let us stop. In other words, admit nothing that can be doubted. Make no assumptions, and take no step which is not compelled by rigorous logic. And, above all, let no feeling or sentiment or desire have any voice in determining belief. If we follow this rule we shall never be confounded, and knowledge will progress.

Opposed to this conception of method is another, as follows: Instead of doubting everything that can be doubted, let us rather doubt nothing until we are compelled to doubt. Let us assume that everything is what it reports itself until some reasons for doubt appear. In society we get on better by assuming that men are truthful, and by doubting only for special reasons, than we should if we assumed that all men are liars, and believed them only when compelled. So in all investigation we make more progress if we assume the truthfulness of the universe and of our own nature than we should if we doubted both.

Such are the two methods. The former assumes everything to be false until proved true; the latter assumes everything to be true until proved false. All fruitful work proceeds upon the latter method; most speculative criticism and closet-philosophy proceed upon the former. Hence their perennial barrenness.

§ 7. The first method seems the more rigorous, but it can be applied only to mathematics, which is purely a subjective science. When we come to deal with reality the method brings thought to a standstill. At the beginning of the modern era, Descartes pretended to doubt everything, and found only one unshakable fact—I think; therefore, I am. But from this he could deduce nothing. The bare fact, "I think," is philosophically insignificant. What I think, or how I think, whether rightly or wrongly, is the important matter. But from the bare "I think" Descartes could reach neither the world of things, nor the world of persons, nor the world of laws. The method was so rigorous as to leave thought without an object. And in general, if we should begin by doubting everything that can be doubted, and by settling all questions in advance, we should never get under way. There are questions in logical theory, in the theory of knowledge, and in metaphysics, which even yet are keenly debated. The sceptic and agnostic and idealist are still abroad.

§ 8. If, then, man were only an abstract speculator, this method of doubting everything which cannot be demonstrated would condemn the mind to a barren subjectivity. But man is not only, or chiefly, an abstract speculator, he is also a living being, with practical interests and necessities, to which he must adjust himself in order to live at all. It has been one of the perennial shortcomings of intellectualism that man has been considered solely as an intellect or understanding; whereas, he is a great deal more. Man is will, conscience, emotion, aspiration; and these are far more powerful factors than the logical intellect. Hence, in its practical unfolding the mind makes a great variety of practical postulates and assumptions which are not logical deductions or speculative necessities, but a kind of *modus vivendi* with the universe. They represent the conditions of our fullest life; and are at bottom expressions of our practical and ideal interests or necessities. And these are reached as articulate principles, not by speculative construction, but by analysis of practical life. Life is richer and deeper than speculation, and contains implicitly the principles by which we live. The law the logician lays down is this: Nothing may be believed which is not proved. The law the mind actually follows is this: Whatever the mind demands for the satisfaction of its subjective interests and tendencies may be assumed as real in default of positive disproof. We propose to trace this principle in the realm of cognition as being the realm which is commonly supposed to be free from all subjective elements.

§ 9. As cognitive beings we desire to know. But reality as it is given to us in immediate experience is not adapted to the needs of our intelligence, and we proceed to work it over so as to make it amenable to our mental necessities. This working over constitutes what we call theoretical science. To do it we tacitly assume that the vast collection of things and events fall into fixed classes, are subject to fixed laws, and are bound up into a rational system.

We assume, further, the essential truthfulness of nature, so that the indications of all clearly determined facts can be trusted. We assume, once more, that nature is not only essentially comprehensible, but that it is comprehensible by us; so that what our nature calls for to make the facts intelligible to *us* is necessary to the facts themselves. For, after all, our explanation of facts always consists in saying that if we may assume certain facts we can understand the actual facts. Thus back of the real universe of experience we construct an ideal universe of the intellect, and we understand the former through the latter. In this way we reach two entirely different conceptions of things. One is furnished by the senses; the other is reached by thought. The former represents reality as it reports itself; the latter represents reality as made over by the mind.

And this is not all. For soon the ideal universe passes for the real, while the real universe of experience is degraded into a phenomenon or appearance. Nothing is allowed to be what it reports itself. All the senses are flouted. The reports of the unsophisticated consciousness are derided. Numberless worlds are invented; a whole family of ethers is generated; and the oddest things are said about everything, as if our aim were to give the lie direct to every spontaneous conviction of common-sense. The doctrines of astronomy, and the current theories of heat, light, sound, and matter are examples. All of these things are, without exception, a series of ideal constructions by which we seek to interpret the reality of experience and make it amenable to our intelligence.

If now we ask for the source and warrant of this theoretic activity we must finally find it in the living interests of our cognitive nature. The facts themselves are indifferent alike to comprehension and non-comprehension. But we seek to comprehend as a matter of course, and take for granted that we have a right to comprehend, that the universe is comprehensible, and that we are able to comprehend it. The assumptions we make are so natural that they even seem necessary truths at times; but in fact they are primarily but projections upon reality of our mental nature and our subjective interests. That conception of a crystalline system of law is purely a subjective ideal and is not known to be an objective fact. The comprehensible universe

is as pure an assumption as the religious and
moral universe. Moreover, the actual universe,
that is the universe as given in experience, is
not intelligible; it is that other assumed ideal
universe, which we have put behind the real
universe, which is intelligible. From a strictly
logical and critical standpoint the intelligible
universe is purely an idol of the human tribe;
nevertheless we insist upon its reality because
the admission of an essentially irrational and
incogitable world violates our cognitive instincts,
throws the mind back upon itself without an
object and without meaning, and leaves it a
prey to scepticism and despair.

§ 10. The existence of this assumptive element
may be further shown by adopting a suggestion
of Arthur Balfour in his "Defence of Philosophic Doubt," and constructing a refutation of
science on the model of the familiar refutation
of religion. We need only demand that the scientist prove his postulates and demonstrate his
assumptions to put him in a sad plight. (1.) Let
him settle with the philosophic sceptic. (2.) Let
him rout the agnostic. (3.) Let him put the
idealist to flight. (4.) Let him prove that a sys-

2

tem of law exists in objective fact. (5.) Let him show that what he needs to comprehend the facts is necessary to the facts themselves. (6.) Let him clear up the difficulties in his own metaphysics. Action at a distance, the nature of the ether, and the relations of matter and force would be good points to begin with. (7.) Let him show that our desire to have the universe comprehensible proves that it is so, or that our unwillingness to admit an irrational reality is any argument against it. (8.) Let him remember that the scientific interest which is so strong in him is very limited indeed, so that it must seem like extreme arrogance on his part to seek to impose the tenets of his little sect upon the universe as necessary laws of the same.

When all these demands have been met there can be some talk about science, but not before. As long as the sceptic and agnostic are abroad there is no security that science is not sheer fiction. As long as the idealist is not silenced, it is doubtful whether even the objects of science exist. If the system of law is not proved to exist, the deductions from it are worthless. Until we prove that what we need to understand the facts is necessary to the facts themselves, our theorizing may be only a projection upon the outer world of our mental nature, and in no way an apprehension of objective reality. As to the metaphysics of science, it is well known to contain difficulties equal to any in theology. So far from answering these questions the average scientist has never heard of them, and yet they seem to concern the life of science itself. The truth is, we meet here the opposition of method to which we referred at the start. The critic affects to doubt whatever cannot be proved, while the scientist takes for granted what every one admits.

§ 11. The sum is this: The mind is not a disinterested logic-machine, but a living organism, with manifold interests and tendencies. These outline its development, and furnish the driving power. The implicit aim in mental development is to recognize these interests, and make room for them, so that each shall have its proper field and object. In this way a series of ideals arise in our mental life. As cognitive, we assume that the universe is rational. Many of its elements are opaque, and utterly unmanageable by us at present, but we assume spontaneously and unconsciously that at the centre all is order, and that there all is crystalline and transparent to intelligence. Thus there arises in our thought the conception of a system in which all is light, a system whose foundations are laid in harmony, and whose structure is rational law, a system every part of which is produced and maintained and illumined by the majestic and eternal Reason. But this is only a cognitive ideal, to which experience yields but little support. But we hold fast the ideal and set aside the facts which make against it as something not yet comprehended.

But we are moral beings also, and our moral interests must be recognized. Hence arises a moral ideal, which we join to the cognitive. The universe must be not only rational, but righteous at its root. Here too we set aside the facts which make against our faith as something not yet understood. This is especially the case in dealing with the problem of evil. Here we are never content with finding a cause for the good and evil in experience; we insist upon an explanation which shall save the assumed goodness at the heart of things.

Finally, we are religious, and our entire nature works together to construct the religious ideal. The intellect brings its ideal; and the conscience brings its ideal; and the affections bring their ideal; and these, together with whatever other thought of perfection we may have, are united into the thought of the one Perfect Being, the ideal of ideals, the supreme and complete, to whom heart, will, conscience, and intellect alike may come and say, "Thy kingdom come; thy will be done." Here, as in the previous cases, we do not ignore the facts which make against the view, but we set them aside as things to be explained, but which must not in any way be allowed to weaken our faith.

All of these ideals are, primarily, alike subjective. They are produced, indeed, under the stress of experience, but they are not transcripts of any possible experience. That transparent universe of the reason is as purely a mental product as that righteous universe of the conscience, or as the supreme perfection of religion. In each of these cases the mind appears with its subjective ideals, and demands that reality shall recognize them; and in all alike reality recognizes them only imperfectly. To some extent the universe is intelligible. To some extent the power not ourselves makes for righteousness. To some extent God is revealed. But in all these cases a purely logical and objective contemplation of the known facts would leave us in great uncertainty. The assured conviction we have rests upon no logical deduction from experience, but upon the optimistic assumption that the mind has a right to itself, and is at home in the universe. The mind will not consent to abandon its nature and resign itself to utter mental and moral confusion. This is, to be sure, an act of pure faith, but it is an act upon which our entire mental life depends. A purely speculative knowledge of reality, which shall be strictly deductive and free from assumption, is impossible.

This result is nothing novel. In principle it coincides with the claim of many of the scholastic theologians, that faith precedes knowledge. The faith-philosophy of Jacobi, the primacy of the practical reason in the Kantian system, and the "pectoral theology" of Schleiermacher are other illustrations of the same view.

§ 12. What, then, of scepticism? Nothing. Specific scepticism, founded on specific reasons, is always respectable, and is but a case of rational criticism; but professional scepticism, based on the bare possibility of doubting, is at once barren and contemptible. It is largely the outcome of mental indolence, and results in mental impotence. This impotent inability to reach a conclusion, so far from being a mark of mental acuteness, is distinctly pathologic. It is not rational, but rather the abdication of reason. As such it is not amenable to reason. It may do individuals damage who are mentally debilitated, but in the development of the race it is of no importance. Universal scepticism is none; for being impartially distributed over the entire mind, it leaves everything just where it was before. Besides, such scepticism is never more than a pretence. But partial scepticism, on a foundation of universal scepticism, is pure arbitrariness, and is at once irrational and unrighteous. To doubt such things as we personally dislike is caprice; to doubt everything is falsehood and pretense.

The fundamental interests of the mind have always secured their recognition. From the beginning the philosophic sceptics have raged and have imagined many bright, and more vain, things; but the burden of their cry has always been, "You cannot prove that you have a right to do what you are doing." But this barren doubt has been ignored, practically by common sense, and theoretically by earnest thinkers, who, having once admitted that it is always abstractly possible, and having seen that it is eternally empty, imitate priest and Levite, and pass by on the other side. The mind is sure to conceive the universe so as to provide for its own interests. So long as any fundamental interest is overlooked or ignored, there can be no peace. Sometimes the intellect has taken things too easy, and has satisfied itself with simple and compendious explanations, which left no place for heart and conscience, and ran off into dry and barren atheisms and materialisms. But before long the rising tides of life and feeling compelled it to try again. On the other hand religion has often made the mistake of denying intellect and conscience their full rights; and forthwith they began their crusade for recognition. Conscience alone has proved a sturdy disturber in theological systems, and one great source and spring of theological progress has been the need of finding a conception of God which the moral nature could accept. As the inner life has grown more complex in manifestation, and richer in content, the system of conceptions has progressed to correspond. It is by this contact with life and reality that thought grows, and not by a barren logic-chopping or verbal haggling about proof. Thus science, ethics, and religion grow; and the mind, in its increasing sense of self-possession and of harmony with the reality of things, becomes more and more indifferent to the objections of the sceptic, and works with ever-growing faith to build up the temple of science, of conscience, and of God.

§ 13. To adjust ourselves to the universe, and the universe to ourselves, so that each shall correspond to the other, we have said, is the implicit aim of mental development; and the law which the mind implicitly follows is this : Whatever our total nature calls for may be assumed as real in default of positive disproof. This gives rise, we have seen, to a variety of practical postulates, which are born of life and not of speculation.

What, now, is the function of logic with regard to these postulates. Plainly not to prove them, but to bring them and their implications out into clear consciousness, and to keep them from losing their way. These postulates themselves are not primarily known as such, but exist rather as implicit tendencies than as clearly defined principles. In this state they readily miss their proper aim. Thus the scientific or cognitive consciousness is a comparatively recent development; and its implications are very imperfectly understood. What is involved in the assumed possibility of objectively valid knowledge is a question rarely asked, and still more rarely answered. Hence, by the grace of ignorance, many a theory lives along in good and regular speculative standing which, if understood, would be seen to destroy knowledge altogether. The farce in such cases is as if one should regard himself as the only existence, and should insist on proving it to his neighbors; but, thanks to logical dulness and flabbiness, it is not perceived. The ethical consciousness, in like manner, is rarely in full possession of itself, and consequently many ethical theories acquire currency, which, if developed into their consequences, would prove fatal to all ethics. The re-

ligious nature also is developed into self-possession only by a long mental labor and experience
extending over centuries. Left to itself it may
fail utterly of comprehending its own implications, and may even lose itself in irreligious assumptions. In all of these fields, therefore, there
is need of a critical procedure which shall aim
to secure consistency in the development of our
postulates, and to adjust their mutual relations.
If we assume a rational and righteous universe,
we must make no assumptions incompatible
therewith. In particular, such a critical procedure is needed to restrain the fanaticism and
insolence of the intellect. This faculty, unless
restrained by criticism, tends to become impa-
tient and overbearing. In its determination to
have a theory it often ignores facts or distorts
them. In this way rationalism has become a
synonym for all that is most superficial and
purblind in speculation. Here, then, is a field
for logic; and here logic has its inalienable
rights. And in this process of inner development, adjustment, and rectification, logic is
equally the servant of cognition, of ethics, and
of religion; while all alike are, fundamentally,
the outgrowths and expressions of our subjec-

tive needs and tendencies as evoked by our total experience.

It would, then, be a complete misunderstanding of our aim to suppose that we are engaging in a polemic against logic and metaphysics. That they are not positively sufficient to give us the principles of practical life is clear, but they do not forbid us to make practical postulates, provided we recognize them in their practical character, and do not proclaim them as demonstrated. But nothing can warrant us in contradicting logic and metaphysics, and no such contradiction can escape final destruction. The lack of proof may be atoned for by practical necessity, but disproof can never be ignored or set aside by any sentiment. Such a difficulty arises in the field of the logical understanding, and there only can it be met. The failure to distinguish the lack of proof from disproof has led to many unwise utterances on the part of some religious teachers. They have proclaimed an independence of both logic and metaphysics, and a complete indifference to their conclusions. Sometimes they have even proclaimed a contradiction between speculation and religion, apparently to show the strength of their own faith.

Such a view must lead either to complete speculative scepticism, or to a civil war among the faculties of the soul; and in either case the result would not be religiously desirable. In other words a mental inventory reveals several classes of propositions: First, some which we must believe; second, some which we must not believe; and third, some which we may believe or assume. Whatever conflicts with the first two classes must be abandoned, and sooner or later will be. It is only in the third class that our interests or desires can have any vote; but this class contains most of what is valuable in life and conduct.

Let us further admit, or rather affirm, that the necessity of passing over difficulties, and taking so much for granted, is not the ideal order of life. The cognitive ideal no doubt involves the speculative solution of all problems, so that our entire thought-system may be perfectly transparent to intelligence. But this ideal is unattainable at present, owing to our limitations. In every department our knowledge is patchwork, and rests on assumption. And, since this is so, it is well to recognize it in order that we may not delude ourselves with a false show of logical rigor, or do injustice to the demands of practical life.

§ 14. These facts in the natural history of belief must be borne in mind if we would understand our mental procedure and development. They explain how it is that we have many beliefs which are not held because we have proved them, but which we try to prove because we hold them. They also explain the barrenness of purely logical criticism. Further, they throw light on the peculiar variations of belief to which all are subject. Since the roots of belief often lie in the sub-logical realm of emotion, sentiment, aspiration, our conviction will vary as the tides of life and feeling rise and fall. A quickening of conscience, a kindling of affection, the loss of a friend, may do more for conviction than volumes of speculation.

Further, it is plain that all thought of strict demonstration must be given up. Demonstration is necessarily confined to the subjective and logical relations of ideas, and can never attach to reality without some element of assumption. But this is as true for physical science as it is for religion. And, in any case, there is no such thing as an objective and self-sufficient demonstration. Truth, as such, is not dependent on demonstration, but exists eternally in its own right. Demonstration is only a makeshift for helping ignorance to insight. It is a stimulus to the mind of the learner to think in certain ways which shall lead him, at last, to see the truth proposed. But such demonstration is conditioned not only by the nature of the stimulus, but also and especially by the development of the mind to which it is addressed. And when we come to an argument in which the whole nature is addressed, the argument must seem weak or strong according as the nature is feebly, or fully, developed. The moral argument for theism cannot seem strong to one without a conscience. The argument from cognitive interests will be empty when there is no cognitive interest. Little souls find very little that calls for explanation or that excites surprise; and they are satisfied with a correspondingly small view of life and existence. In such a case we cannot hope for universal agreement. We can only proclaim the faith that is in us, and the reasons for it, in the hope that reality may not utterly reject it, and that the faith in question may not be without some response in other minds and hearts. Faith and unfaith alike can do no more; and the survival of the fittest must decide between them.

This renunciation of demonstration has been distasteful to many, but needlessly. In any case it has to be made. We cannot make an argument a demonstration by calling it such; and, besides, the force of an argument in no way depends on its name, but on its logic. But the chief ground of trouble seems to lie in a psychological oversight. If a proposition is not demonstrated, then it is at best only probable, and, if probable, then uncertain. Hence, to renounce demonstration is to hand the subject over to uncertainty, and who can live on uncertainties? The next thing is to call God a "perhaps," and the shortcomings of natural theology stand revealed. But such utterances tacitly assume that belief is always the product of logic. But life abounds in practical certainties for which no very cogent reasons can be given, but which are nevertheless the foundation of daily life. Our practical trust in the uniformity of nature, in one another, in the affection of friends, in the senses, etc., are examples. Numberless logical objections could be raised which reduce all of these to matters of probability; but none of these things move us. The things which we hold, or rather which hold us, with deepest conviction are, not the certainties of logic, but of life.

§ 15. Theistic discussion has been largely confined to the one question of the divine intelligence. The narrowness of such a view and its sure failure to reach a properly religious conception are already apparent. This limitation of the argument has several grounds :

(1.) The question of intelligence is basal; and everything else stands or falls with it. Hence, the question between theism and atheism has been generally conceived as a question between intelligence and non-intelligence as the ground of the universe.

(2.) This question can be debated largely on the basis of objective facts. It seems, therefore, to involve fewer subjective elements, such as appeals to conscience and feeling, and hence it furnishes more common ground for the disputants than the other arguments.

(3.) The argument has seemed religiously ade-

3

quate, because the theist has generally had the Christian conception of God in his mind; and hence when some degree of skill and contrivance was shown in the world about us, this conception, together with the ideal tendency of the soul, at once came in to expand this poor result into the ideal religious form.

§ 16. But, in spite of the previous strictures, most of our time will be devoted to discussing the question of intelligence *versus* non-intelligence. The idea of God may be treated from a double standpoint, metaphysical and religious. In the former, God appears as the principle of knowing and explanation. In the latter, he is the implication of the religious consciousness, or that without which that consciousness would fall into discord with itself. The former view does not attain to any distinctly religious conception, but it furnishes elements which must enter into every religious conception. Hence, in any study of the subject, it can never be needless, though it may be incomplete. Opposing errors are traditional here. On the one hand, mere reasoning has been made all-sufficient, and a very dry and barren rationalism has been the result. On the other hand, feeling has been made supreme, and the just claims of intellect have been ignored. This has often gone to the extent of basing religion on speculative scepticism; but though the lion and the lamb have been induced to lie together for a while, it has always ended in the lion's making way with the lamb. On a subject of such importance we cannot have too many allies. It does not weaken the argument from feeling and aspiration to show that the pure intellect also demands and implies God. Our preliminary work will deal chiefly with the intellectual aspects of the question, though we reserve the right to appeal to the emotional nature upon occasion.

From the side of pure intellect, also, the theistic question can take on two forms. We can seek to show (1) that the order of the world cannot be understood without intelligence as its cause, and (2) that reason itself falls into discord and despair without God. In the former case God appears as a necessary hypothesis for the understanding of the facts; in the latter case God appears as a necessary implication of the rational life. Of course such an aim implies that the laws of thought are objectively valid;

that over against the subjective necessities of thought are corresponding objective necessities of being; but this assumption underlies the whole system of objective knowledge, and is not peculiar to theism. The only rational aim must be to show that the mind being as it is, and experience being as it is, the belief in God is a necessary implication of both. If this aim should be attained, then every one would have to decide for himself whether to accept his nature with its implications and indications, or to abandon it arbitrarily and capriciously. If, however, any one does choose the part of the irrationalist, it is hoped that he will consistently retire into silence, and not mortify earnest thinkers by the assumption of superior insight, nor weary them by his dreary and monotonous outcry.

§ 17. Finally, a word of a pedagogical character must be allowed. Owing to certain instinctive prejudices of common-sense, theism is often unfairly dealt with. In particular it is often tacitly assumed that matter and force, and with them atheism, have the field, and must be allowed to remain in possession until they are driven off. Thus theism is branded as an hypothesis, and is called upon to prove a negative; while atheism is supposed to express the fact of experience, and to need no further proof. Hence the failure of theism to demonstrate its position is oddly enough regarded as establishing atheism. Every one acquainted with atheistic treatises will recognize that their chief force has been in picking flaws in the theistic argument. There has been comparatively little effort to show any positive sufficiency of atheism to give any rational account of the facts.

Such a position is infantile in the extreme; it properly belongs to the palæontological period of speculation. The nature of reality is a thought-problem; and our thought of reality is the solution of that problem. Whether we think of it as one or many, material or immaterial, the theory is equally speculative in each case; its value must be decided by its adequacy to the facts. If theism is an hypothesis, atheism is no less so. If theism is a theory or speculation, atheism is equally so. The candid mind must seek to judge between them. This can be done only as we put both views alongside of the facts and of each other, and choose the simpler and

more rational.   No theory can be judged by its
ability to make grimaces at opposing views, but
only by its own positive adequacy to the facts.
The theistic theory, with all its difficulties, must
be put alongside of the atheistic theory with all
its difficulties.   When this is done the theist
will have little cause to blush for his credulity,
or to be ashamed of his faith.

Another common error must be noted.   When
we come to the deepest questions of thought
we always come upon impenetrable mystery.
We have to affirm facts whose possibility we
cannot construe.   We have to make admissions
which we cannot further deduce nor comprehend.   In unclear and untaught minds this is
often made a stumbling-block; and the fancy
gets abroad that theism is an especially difficult
doctrine.   In truth, all science and all thought
are full of what has been called limit-notions;
that is, notions which the facts force upon us,
and which are perfectly clear from the side of
the facts, but which from the farther side are
lost in difficulty and mystery.   They express
an ultimate affirmation along a given line of
thought, and can never be grasped from the farther side.   When taken out of their relations,

or when we seek to comprehend them without remembering the law of their formation, nothing is easier than to make them seem contradictory or absurd. But theism must not be held responsible for all the difficulties of metaphysics; and in particular we must be careful in escaping one difficulty that we do not fall into a greater. The notion of an eternal person, an unbegun consciousness, is at least no more difficult than the alternative notion of eternal matter and unbegun motion. It is not the mark of a high grade of intelligence to take offence at the difficulties of a given view, and end by adopting another still more obnoxious to criticism.

We do not propose, then, to prove the divine existence, but rather to propose a solution of the problem which the world and life force upon us. We have no expectation of clearing up all the puzzles of metaphysics. We simply hope to show that without a theistic faith we must stand as dumb and helpless before the deeper questions of thought and life as a Papuan or Patagonian before an eclipse.

CHAPTER I.

THE UNITY OF THE WORLD-GROUND.

§ 18. KANT has grouped the leading theistic arguments into three: ontological, cosmological, and physico-theological, and has made each the subject of a special criticism. In this, along with much that is incisive and final, there is also much that is arbitrary and verbal. His discussion, as a whole, is somewhat antiquated, and is conducted throughout on Kantian principles. The argument from design fails to reach the full idea of God; and the notion of a necessary and perfect being upon which the other arguments depend is a subjective ideal of the reason. His criticism rests on two pillars: (1) the traditional prejudice of intellectualism that demonstration is necessary to belief, and (2) the Kantian principle that the forms and ideals of the reason have no objective significance. Both of these views are outgrown. Nowadays only belated minds expect demonstration in any department of objective knowledge. It is evident, also, that all thinking, and hence all knowing, must be conditioned by our mental nature. In no way can the mind get outside of itself and grasp things otherwise than through the conceptions which its nature allows it to form. But this necessary subjectivity of all knowledge is compatible with the view that there is a harmony between the nature of thought and the nature of things. Such harmony cannot, indeed, be demonstrated; but no one can help practically assuming it to some extent. It is dreary and profitless labor, therefore, to dwell upon the subjectivity of knowledge. The mind has always insisted on attributing objective validity or universality to some of its subjective factors; and fruitful criticism must be restricted to inquiring which subjective elements have objective value. No one has insisted more strongly than Kant on the necessity of theism as an implication of reason; but the exigencies of his system led him to deny this fact any further significance.

§ 19. Since in discussing the question our aim must be to produce conviction, it is important (1) to find some admitted fact or principle as a

point of departure, and (2) not to attempt to
do too much at once. Such a point is not furnished by either the ontological or the design
argument.

The ontological argument in its common form
rests on the notion of the perfect being. But
the idea of the perfect necessarily includes the
idea of existence, and would be a contradiction
without it. Hence it has been concluded that
the perfect exists. But there is not a shadow
of cogency in this reasoning. It only points
out that the idea of the perfect must include
the idea of existence; but there is nothing to
show that the self-consistent idea represents an
objective reality. Hence Descartes sought to
supplement the argument by showing that only
the perfect can be the source of the idea. In
fact the argument is nothing but the expression of the æsthetic and ethical conviction that
the true, the beautiful, and the good, which alone
have value in the universe, cannot be foreign to
the universe. The mind will not consent to
abandon its ideals. The ontological argument
owes all its force to this immediate faith in the
ideal. Its technical expression is due to the
desire to give this faith a demonstrative logical

form. The result is to weaken rather than strengthen it.

The teleological or design argument is based upon the purpose - like adaptations which are found, especially in the organic world. This has always been a favorite with the Anglo-Saxon mind; and Kant mentions it with great respect. Whatever its logical faults and speculative shortcomings, it is better adapted to convince common-sense than the more speculative arguments. Still, when taken strictly, it is open to so many critical objections, and the affirmed design in nature is so much in dispute, that, in the present state of thought, it does not offer the best starting-point for the discussion. Thus the great mass of natural products look more like effects than purposes. In the various disposition of natural agents, of land and water, of mountain and plain, etc., there may be purpose; but to observation they seem to be simple facts from which certain results follow. Again, in the relation of the organic and the inorganic, there may be purpose; but the fact of observation is that the latter is usable by the former, not that it was made for it. If the intelligence of the world-ground were otherwise and elsewhere

demonstrated, there is much in the relation of
these two worlds which would illustrate that
intelligence; but there is not much that can be
used as original proof. It is in the organic
world that we find unambiguous marks of adaptation; but here, unfortunately, the most of the
ends realized do not seem worth realizing. They
have no manifest value or reason, but are just
such meaningless things as we should expect if
an irrational power were at work. Had not
our idea of God been otherwise determined,
these things would prove less a help than an
embarrassment. Again, allowing the existence
of design in nature, this argument by no means
justifies us in affirming a single cause of the
world. A polytheistic conception remains possible; and, considering the antitheses of good
and evil, of sense and nonsense in nature, such
a view would accord only too well with experience. Christianity has accustomed us to monotheism, but in strict logic the design argument,
on the basis of experience, would have difficulty
in making it out. The argument seems sufficient because, in its common use, it is not a
deduction of the theistic idea, but only an illustration of the theistic faith which we already

possess. It seems well, therefore, to look for some other starting-point; and this must be sought in some form of the cosmological argument.

This argument has had a fixed aim rather than a constant form. The aim is to pass from the cosmos as a contingent and conditioned existence to the affirmation of a necessary and unconditioned existence. The form of the argument has been various. Sometimes the argument has been from motion to an unmoved prime mover; sometimes from secondary causes to an uncaused first cause; sometimes from contingent existence to necessary existence, or from dependent existence to independent existence. In its traditional forms the argument is open to many objections. We shall do better, therefore, to change the form and to lower the aim. Instead, then, of seeking to establish the full religious conception of God at once, we content ourselves with the humbler aim of showing that the ground of all reality, or the fundamental reality, or the world-ground, must be one and not many.

§ 20. In this claim we are in harmony with the great majority of thinkers, both of ancient

and modern times. Even theistic and non-theistic thinkers have agreed in rejecting a fundamental pluralism in favor of a basal monism.
The most pronounced non-theistic and atheistic
schemes of our time label themselves monism,
although not always showing the clearest appreciation of what true monism means and requires.
Even Kant, who will not allow any objective
validity to knowledge, insists that monism is
the deepest demand of the reason.

But while there is agreement in the fact, there
is much diversity in the modes of reaching it.
And here it is that we need to find the best
point of departure, and one which will command
universal assent. Leibnitz and Lotze have found
this in the fact of interaction. This fact, when
unfolded, is seen to imply the unity of the
world-ground. We shall do better, perhaps, to
make the postulates of objective cognition our
starting-point; but of these interaction is one
of the chief. The view may be expounded as
follows:

All investigation of the world of reality rests
upon certain postulates, and is absurd without
them. These are interaction, law, and system.
The first implies that things mutually affect or

determine one another. Without this assumption any event would be an absolute and unrelated beginning. The universe would fall asunder into disconnected and uncaused units, and the individual consciousness would be shut up within itself. Again, it implies that all things interact; for if there were anything out of all relations of causation, it would be for us a figment of the imagination.

But interaction alone would not suffice; for there might be irregular interaction. There is no law of reason which assures us that all being and action must be absolutely determined. Such irregular action would meet the demands of causation, but not of cognition; hence we must next add the idea of uniformity, or that under the same circumstances the same thing will always occur.

But this implies, further, a universal adjustment of everything to every other, such that for a given state of one there can be only a given state of the rest fixed both in kind and degree. Without this assumption unlike causes would have like effects, and like causes would have unlike effects, and there could be no thought of theoretical cognition. There must be, then, interaction and law among things; and these things cannot be and do what they choose, but all must be bound up in a common scheme; that is, there must be system.

These postulates command universal assent as the basis of all objective cognition. They are not doubted like the assumption of design, but are implied in the very structure of knowledge. The specific nature of the laws and the system is, indeed, a problem for solution; but the existence of rational law and system is implicitly assumed.

Our starting-point, then, is the conception of things interacting according to law, and forming an intelligible system. The advantage, however, lies in its general acceptance, and not in its being speculatively demonstrated. Critically considered, the universe, or nature, as system is an ideal of the cognitive nature as God is an ideal of the religious nature, while neither admits of proper demonstration. But for one reason or another cognitive ideals are more easily accepted than religious ideals, and hence we start with the former, and proceed to develop their implications.

4

§ 21. In a complete discussion of interaction many points would have to be dwelt upon which we pass over here. Our present concern is to show that such a system of interacting members cannot be construed by thought without the assumption of a unitary being, which is the fundamental reality of the system. How is a unitary system of interacting members possible? This is the problem. Only through a unitary being which posits and maintains them in their mutual relations. This is the solution.

Spontaneous thought posits all its objects as real, and finds no reason for not thinking them mutually independent. They all seem to exist together in space, and no one seems to imply any other. In this stage of thought it is easy to believe that things are mutually indifferent and independent, so that any one would continue to exist if all the rest should fall away. But this fancy is banished by the rise of reflective thought. Physical science has made us familiar with the relativity of all physical existence. The elements have not their properties or forces absolutely and in themselves, but only in their relations or as members of the system. They are all conditioned in their activities, and

hence conditioned in their being; for metaphysics shows that conditioned activity implies
conditioned being. In practice we get over the
difficulty by treating of the laws of the elements, which always imply relations and conditions. The ontological question is ignored. In
this way we practically recognize the conditioned nature of things, while the spontaneous
fancy of a self-sufficient being in all things lives
along undisturbed in the background of our
thought.

The attempts to explain interaction are manifold, but they all fail as long as the things
are left independent. Most attempts, indeed,
are only figures of speech. Thus an influence
is said to pass; but this only describes the fact,
for an influence is nothing which can exist apart
from its subject. The physicists, again, speak
of forces which play between things; but this
returns to the previous view. For forces are
only abstractions from the activities of things,
and hence cannot pass between things. The fact
of observation is simply that mutual changes
are observed among things. To explain these
we say that things act upon or determine one
another. To explain this fact we next posit

forces in the things; and this is either to re-
name the problem or else to fall back into the
notion of influence. Finally, some have sought
to dispense with these forces, and explain all
interaction as the result of impact, thinking that
action at a distance is the great difficulty. This
view limits the problem to the physical field,
and is a double failure even there.

First, the theory of impact cannot be carried
through in physical science; and second, action
by impact is no more intelligible between independent things than action at a distance. The
separation in space does not make the difficulty,
but only enables the imagination to grasp it.
But if things be independent, that is, be what
they are without reference to anything else,
there is no reason why one thing should in any
way be affected by any other. Such beings, if
in space, would be as indifferent when in the
same point as when separated by the infinite
void.

The notion of interaction implies that a thing
is determined by others, and hence that it cannot be all that it is apart from all others. If
all its activities and properties are conditioned,
it implies that the thing cannot exist at all out

of its relations. Its existence is involved in its relations, and would vanish with them. The notion of independence, on the other hand, implies that the thing is not determined by others, but has the ground of all its determinations in itself. These two notions are distinct contradictions. No passage of influences or forces will avail to bridge the gulf as long as the things are regarded as independent. There is no escape from denying either the independence or the interaction.

Let us affirm the independence. Then we have the conception of an indefinite plurality of things, each of which is self-existent and self-sufficient, but which perpetually changes, however, in accordance with corresponding changes in every other. These mutual changes form, apparently, a system of interaction according to law; and yet it has no ground in the mutual relations of things, but simply is. Applied to perception, it would imply that each mind develops its world of things and persons out of itself, and without any stimulus from reality beyond itself.

This view no one has ever ventured to hold. The developed mind will never consent to believe that absolute and essentially unrelated existences can fit into and form a system. The harmony itself is a problem for which the mind insists on demanding a solution. The farthest thought can go in affirming the independence of these apparently interacting things is to make them mutually independent, while all alike depend on a higher reality, which is the ground both of their existence and of their harmony. This is the view of Liebnitz as expressed in his monadology and pre-established harmony. Concerning the truth of this view we need pronounce no opinion. It suffices to have shown that it must have recourse to a unitary world-ground.

Let us next try the opposite view, that things do really interact or mutually determine one another. We have already seen that the popular view, in which things exist in a hard and fast self-identity and self-sufficiency, must be given up. All these things must be reduced to a relative and dependent existence. Where, then, is the absolute and independent existence? At first we are tempted to say that the system itself is that existence; but the system itself, apart from its conditioned members, is nothing.

By hypothesis these members, *A*, *B*, *C*, etc., are the only ontological realities; and the system is only our conception of their relations. But we cannot rest in them, for *A* refers us to *B*, and *B* to *C*, and we reach no resting-place. We cannot rest in the members taken singly, for each refers us to all the others. We cannot rest in the sum of the members, for a sum, as such, is only a mental product; and we get no hint of what it is in reality which is able to add a series of dependent units in so potent a fashion as to bring out an independent sum. For the same reason we cannot rest in the system; for the system is only a conception. To rest in the system we must make it the ontological reality, and regard the members only as its implications or phases. Instead of constructing the system from the members as ontological units, we must rather construct the members from the system.

Here Kant may tell us that we are pursuing a shadow of our own reason. We reply that the only question which can rationally be raised in this field is, How must we think about the fundamental reality? And we hold that the mind cannot rest in the thought of a fundamental pluralism. Only two conceptions are

possible.   We may think of A, B, C, etc., as dependent on some one being, M, distinct from
them which co-ordinates them and mediates
their interaction.   Or we may think of them, not
as dependent on something outside of them, but
on some one being in them which is their reality,
and of which they are in some sense but phases
or modifications.   Things, in the common use
of the term, would have but derived or phenomenal reality, and would have even this existence
only in and through the one fundamental reality.
The decision between these two views must be
left for future study; but both alike compel the
denial of the self-sufficiency of things and the
affirmation of a unitary world-ground.   And to
this being we give the name of infinite and absolute.   This does not imply that it is the all,
but only that it is the independent ground of
the finite.   No more does it imply that it is out
of all relations, but only that it is out of all
restrictive relations to anything beyond itself,
and is the independent source of the finite and
all its relations.

§ 22. The argument thus outlined is open to
many scruples, but, I believe, to no valid objec-

tions. The scruples are largely born of our general bondage to the senses. For one who supposes that the senses give immediate and final metaphysical insight the argument will have no force. But we have no desire to convince such a one. Even wisdom is justified only of her children. It is possible to come to any argument with so undeveloped a mental retina as to make vision impossible. But I am persuaded that, apart from these pathological cases, when we become familiar with the terms and their meaning, and also with the inner structure of reason, we shall see that the mind can rest in no other conclusion.

We replace, then, the pluralism of spontaneous thought by a basal monism. Of course this view does not remove all difficulties, nor answer all questions. On the contrary, it leaves the mystery of being as dark and opaque as ever. Its only value lies in giving expression to the mind's demand for ultimate unity, and in removing the contradiction which lies in the assumption of interaction between independent things. But we cannot pretend to picture to ourselves the relations of the infinite and the finite, nor to construe the possibility of the infinite. We come here to a necessity which meets us everywhere when we touch the frontiers of knowledge — namely, the necessity of admitting facts which, while they must be recognized and admitted, cannot be deduced or comprehended.

Of the nature of the infinite as yet we know only that it is one, and metaphysics compels us to regard it also as active. But this is so far from being the complete idea of God that both atheism and pantheism might accept it. Still we have made some progress. We have reached a point to which the design argument alone could not bring us. It is plain that polytheism is untenable; and that if any kind of theism is to be affirmed it must be monotheism. We attempt, now, some further determinations of our thought of this fundamental being. We hope, at least, to be allowed, if not compelled, to identify the One of speculation with the God of religion.

But before passing to this inquiry a word must be devoted to a traditional verbalism. Is this One, it will be asked, immanent or transcendent? and we might even be instructed that thought can never transcend the universe. We might reply by asking for a definition of the terms. It would be absurd to take them spatially, as if immanent meant inside and transcendent outside; a fancy, however, which seems to underlie not a few utterances on this subject. The One cannot be conceived as the sum of the many, nor as the stuff out of which the many are made, neither does it depend on the many; but, conversely, the many depend on it. In this sense the One is transcendent. Again, the many are not spatially outside of the One, nor a pendulous appendage of the One; but the One is the ever - present power in and through which the many exist. In this sense the One is immanent. In any other sense the terms are words without any meaning.

The alleged impossibility of transcending the universe is another form of the same verbalism. In the sense defined we must transcend it; in any other sense there is no need of transcending it. In modern thought substantiality has been replaced or defined by causality. A world-substance, as distinguished from a world-cause, is a product of the imagination which vanishes before criticism. For the explanation of the system we need a cause which shall not be this, that, or the other thing, but an omnipresent agent by which all things exist. This agent may be called anything, first cause, absolute, infinite, world-ground, or even universe, if only we keep the meaning in mind; and the meaning is that power not ourselves, nor any other finite thing, by which all things exist. If we choose we may unite this agent and all its cosmic products into the one thought of the universe; and we may then loudly proclaim the impossibility of transcending the universe; but this procedure will hardly tend to clearness, as the term universe is generally restricted to mean the system of finite things and manifestations. Still, if any one finds pleasure in teaching that thought is limited to the universe when the universe is taken as the totality of being, it would be hard-hearted, indeed, to deny him this cheap satisfaction.

Perhaps, however, this severity ought to be a little mitigated, for there is a back-lying thought which may be hinted at by this antithesis of immanence and transcendence, although it is not expressed by it. This concerns the question whether the world-ground be fully expressed and exhausted in the world, or whether, apart from the real world, there are infinite possibilities in the nature of the fundamental reality. At bottom this question turns upon the freedom or necessity of the world-ground, and must be postponed for the present.

CHAPTER II.

THE WORLD-GROUND AS INTELLIGENT.

MANY questions might fitly be raised at this point, but we postpone them for the central question of theism — the intelligence of the world-ground. We premise, however, a pair of principles from metaphysics.

1. This world-ground, by its independent position, is the source of the finite and of all its determinations. Whether we view it as blind or seeing, necessitated or free, none the less must we hold that no finite thing has any ground of existence in itself, but that it owes its existence, nature, and history, entirely to the demands which the world-ground makes upon it. If not in the plan, then in the nature of this fundamental reality we must seek the conditioning ground of things.

2. This world-ground is not to be regarded as stuff or raw material, but as cause or agent.

The stuff-notion is a product of the imagination, and vanishes before criticism.

The human mind has only two principles of causal explanation: (1) necessary or mechanical agency, which is driven from behind, and (2) self-directing intelligent agency, which is led from before. Verbal phrases can be constructed to represent other principles, which are neither free nor necessary, neither blind nor seeing; but there is no corresponding thought. The question then becomes, Which of the two principles mentioned offers the best ultimate explanation of the universe, man being included?

Here we might inquire into the relative metaphysical difficulty of the two conceptions. It is commonly supposed that the notion of a self-directing agent has in it very grave, if not insuperable, metaphysical difficulties; but we should find this conception at least no more difficult than the opposite one of an all-embracing necessity. In fact there is nothing positive in the latter notion, and the more we examine it the more elusive and unmanageable it becomes. But we shall do well to avoid these abysses of metaphysics for the present, and take a more familiar road.

The believer in self-directing, self-possessing reason as the only adequate ground of things, offers various reasons for his faith. They are drawn from (1) the order and intelligibility of the universe, (2) the myriad indications of design in things, (3) intelligence in man, and (4) the overthrow of reason and cognition involved in any atheistic and necessitarian scheme. These reasons we now have to expound and consider.

The Argument from Order and Intelligibility.

§ 24. This argument is drawn chiefly from the physical system. In the previous chapter we pointed out that all study of objective reality assumes the fact of law and system, or a universal adjustment of each to all in a common scheme of order. Here we next point out that all study assumes that this system is an intelligible or rational one. A rational cosmos is the implicit assumption of objective cognition. But we have already pointed out, what psychology abundantly demonstrates, that we reach this system, not by a passive reception of ready-made knowledge, but by constructing from the data of experience a series of rational conceptions, and objectifying them as real. The true system is not immediately given in appearances; our knowledge of it arises only as the mind works over the appearances, and projects the resulting conceptions under the form of space, time, substance, causality, and the other categories of thought. But if the knowledge is to have any validity, the laws of thought must be laws of the universe itself. Things which are to be known must exist in intelligible, that is rational, order and relations, and also in profound adjustment to the nature of the mind itself. The problem of human knowledge, then, involves (1) a knowable, that is a rational, universe; (2) a knowing human mind; (3) the identity of the categories of human thought with the principles of cosmic being; (4) such an adjustment of the outer to the inner that the mind, reacting according to its own nature against external stimulus, shall produce in itself thoughts which shall truly reproduce the objective fact, and (5) an identity of rational nature in human beings. If human reason were many, and not one, there would be an end to thought. These implications are so involved in the very structure of knowledge that we take them for granted without thought of their significance;

5

whereas they are the perennial wonder of existence.

If, then, knowledge be possible, we must declare that the world-ground proceeds according to thought-laws and principles, that it has established all things in rational relations, and balanced their interaction in quantitative and qualitative proportion, and measured this proportion by number. "God geometrizes," says Plato. "Number is the essence of reality," says Pythagoras. And to this agree all the conclusions of scientific thought. The heavens are crystallized mathematics. All the laws of force are numerical. The interchange of energy and chemical combination are equally so. Crystals are solid geometry. Many organic products show similar mathematical laws. Indeed, the claim is often made that science never reaches its final form until it becomes mathematical. But simple existence in space does not imply motion in mathematical relations, or existence in mathematical forms. Space is only the formless ground of form, and is quite compatible with the irregular and amorphous. It is equally compatible with the absence of numerical law. The truly mathematical is the work of the spirit.

Hence the wonder that mathematical principles should be so pervasive, that so many forms and processes in the system represent definite mathematical conceptions, and that they should be so accurately weighed and measured by number.

If the cosmos were a resting existence, we might possibly content ourselves by saying that things exist in such relations once for all, and that there is no going behind this fact. But the cosmos is no such rigid monotony of being; it is, rather, a process according to intelligible rules; and in this process the rational order is perpetually maintained or restored. The weighing and measuring continually goes on. In each chemical change just so much of one element is combined with just so much of another. In each change of place the intensities of attraction and repulsion are instantaneously adjusted to correspond. Apart from any question of design, the simple fact of qualitative and quantitative adjustment of all things, according to fixed law, is a fact of the utmost significance. The world-ground works at a multitude of points, or in multitude of things throughout the system, and works in each with exact reference to its activities in all the rest. The displace-

ment of an atom by a hair's-breadth demands a
corresponding readjustment in every other within the grip of gravitation. But all are in constant movement, and hence readjustment is continuous and instantaneous. The single law of
gravitation contains a problem of such dizzy
vastness that our minds faint in the attempt to
grasp it; but when the other laws of force are
added the complexity defies all understanding.
In addition we might refer to the building processes in organic forms, whereby countless struct-
ures are constantly produced or maintained, and
always with regard to the typical form in question. But there is no need to dwell upon this
point.

Here, then, is a problem, and we have only
the two principles of intelligence and non-intelligence, of self-directing reason and blind necessity, for its solution. The former is adequate,
and is not far-fetched and violent. It assimilates
the facts to our own experience, and offers the
only ground of order of which that experience
furnishes any suggestion. If we adopt this view
all the facts become luminous and consequent.

If we take the other view, then we have to
assume a power which produces the intelligible

and rational, without being itself intelligent and rational. It works in all things, and in each with exact reference to all, yet without knowing anything of itself or of the rules it follows, or of the order it founds, or of the myriad products compact of seeming purpose which it incessantly produces and maintains. If we ask why it does this, we must answer, Because it must. If we ask how we know that it must, the answer must be, By hypothesis. But this reduces to saying that things are as they are because they must be. That is, the problem is abandoned altogether. The facts are referred to an opaque hypothetical necessity, and this turns out, upon inquiry, to be the problem itself in another form. There is no proper explanation except in theism.

§ 25. Two causes serve to conceal the weakness of the atheistic explanation :

1. We fancy that we see causes, and especially that we see matter to be a real cause. Spirit, on the other hand, is a purely hypothetical cause, and is assumed only to explain that which the undoubted cause, matter, cannot account for. Hence theism is presented as maintaining a hy-

pothetical cause, God, against a real cause, matter; and as matter is daily found to explain more and more, there is less and less need of God. Here, then, necessity and non-intelligence are manifestly united in most effective causation; and who can set bounds to their possibilities?

This thought has been a leading factor in the atheistic renascence of recent years. The answer must be that it is an echo of an obsolete theory of knowledge. We know directly nothing of causes. We experience certain effects, which we refer to causes; and the nature of the causes is learned by inference from the effects. Matter is not seen to cause anything; nor is spirit seen to cause anything. The cause of cosmic phenomena is hidden from observation; and the only question possible is, How must we think of that cause? Our answer is equally speculative and metaphysical in every case. The theist, observing the law and order among the phenomena, refers them ultimately to a power which knows itself and what it is doing. The atheist refers them to a power which knows nothing of itself or of what it is doing.

2. The second cause which conceals the weakness of this position is found in the notion of

law. The human mind is especially prone to hypostasize abstractions, and subject things to them. The reign of law is a phrase which has thus acquired a purely factitious significance. Law appears as something apart from things, which rules over them and determines all their doings. Thus the law of gravity is conceived of as something separate from things, and to which things are subject; and the mystery of gravitation is removed by calling it a law. The mistake is palpable. Laws have no thing-like existence, but are simply general expressions either of fact or of the rule according to which some agent proceeds. Things do not attract one another because the law of gravitation calls for it; but they attract, and from a comparison of many cases we find that the intensity of this attraction varies according to a certain rule. But this rule does not found the fact; it only expresses it. The same is true for all the other laws of nature. They neither found nor compel the facts, but simply express them. Yet, misled by our persistent tendency to mistake abstractions for things, we first give a kind of substantive character to the laws, and then we carry them behind the things as pre-existent necessities, which explain everything, but which themselves are in no more need of explanation than the self-sufficient and eternal truths of the reason. The untaught mind tends to think under the form of necessity; and this necessity, which is but the mind's own shadow, forthwith passes for an explanation. Thus we reach the grotesque inversion of reason which makes the very fact of rational order a ground for denying a controlling reason.

In fact, however, the laws form a large part of the problem. When we have said that the world-ground co-ordinates things by fixed rules of quantity and quality, and with perfect adaptation and numerical adjustment, we have but stated the problem, not solved it. That the adjustment takes place with consciousness is not seen; that it takes place by necessity is also not seen. Both the consciousness and the necessity are added to the observation. Change according to rule is all that is given. If we ask how this can be, we can only appeal either to intelligence or non-intelligence. Comte says that it is a mark of immaturity to raise this question; but if we will raise it, theism is the only answer. The atheist he pronounces to be the most inconsequent of theologians, since he raises theological questions and rejects the only possible way of dealing with them.

§ 26. The only thing which could justify us in adopting non-intelligence as the ground of the cosmic order, would be to show that the system, with all its laws and members, are rational necessities, or implications of the basal reality. The truths of mathematics are implications of our intuitions of space and number; and for these truths we ask no ground, they being able to stand alone. It is conceivable that in like manner the cosmos, in all its features, should be shown to be an implication of the independent reality which underlies all.

This was once a dream of speculation, and the attempt was made to realize it. Of course it failed. No reflection on the bare notion of independent being gives any insight into the actual order. The basal distinction of matter and spirit we discover, not deduce. The modes of cosmic activity are of the same kind. Any of the cosmic laws, from gravitation on, might conceivably have been lacking or altogether different. And, allowing the laws, their outcome

might have been in all respects different. For
the laws alone do not determine the result, but
only when taken with the conditions under
which they work. Had the conditions been different, the same laws would have produced
other results. But these conditions are all contingent. No trace of necessity can be found in
the cosmos or its laws. They are simply facts
which we recognize without pretending to deduce. Metaphysics might also try to show that
this notion of necessity, when pushed to its results, would cancel the unity of the basal One,
and, instead of landing us on the solid rock,
would leave us in the abysses. But we rest the
argument. Here is a power which works intel-
ligibly and according to law, in which everything is adjusted to everything else with nicest
balance and adaptation, and in which this balance is incessantly reproduced. The theist concludes that this power is intelligent, the atheist
concludes that it is not. The theist holds that
the rational and intelligible work point to reason and intelligence. The atheist concludes that
the rational and intelligible work point to unreason and non-intelligence. Between these two
views each must decide for himself.

In leaving this argument a single vulgar objection must be warded off. It has been said that we cannot conceive that the cosmic processes are carried on by intelligence. This is true enough if it means that we cannot picture the process in detail. We certainly cannot conceive how a mind could conduct the ceaseless and infinitely complex processes of nature without weariness or confusion. To conceive how it could do it we must ourselves be equal to the task. But if it be hard to see how intelligence could do it, it is at least equally so to see how non-intelligence could do it. The alternative lies between the two, with the advantage always in favor of the former. For when we ascribe to the world-ground omnipotence and omniscience, we make at least a formal provision for the case. We can see that such a being would be adequate to the task, and we are under no obligation to tell how he would get on with it. That is his own affair. But with the assertion of the world-ground as non-intelligent, we fail to make even this formal provision, and the facts remain opaque and unintelligible. Our total conclusion from the facts of order, law, and system is that if they are to be explained,

it can be only on a theistic basis. Atheism does
not explain them, but only asserts that they are
facts which are because they must be; and we
know that they must be by hypothesis.

§ 27. We have said that the world-ground must
be intelligent or non-intelligent. This has been
disputed on the ground that intelligence and
non-intelligence do not form a complete disjunc-
tion, so that there may be a third something
higher than either, and transcendental to both.
In our own time, which has a craze for self-
sophistication, this claim has been paraded as
something especially profound, and as vacating
both theism and atheism. The true explanation
of the cosmos is to be found in neither intelligence nor non-intelligence, but in the inscrutable
transcendental. This doctrine has a swelling
sound, but is empty of the slightest substance.
The speculative fancy has been unspeakably
prolific in the production of words for its expression, but they are purely logical sound and
fury, signifying nothing. This transcendental
X is not a thought, but a phrase. It exists solely by the grace of language, which has the un-
fortunate property of making it possible to talk

long and learnedly without saying anything. To appeal to this X is not to explain, but to abandon explanation. Explanation must always be in intelligible terms; and as in our thought the intelligent and the non-intelligent comprise all existence, any true explanation must be in terms of one or the other. $X \, Y \, Z$ may be a very profound truth in the realm of the inscrutable, but in the realm of intelligence it is only a meaningless group of letters.

In one case, however, we can speak of something higher than intelligence. Our thought contains two elements; a certain rational content or insight, and a variety of processes by which this insight is reached. The former is the universal and objective element of thought, the latter may be formal and relative to us. If, now, by intelligence we mean our methods of procedure, the devices of our discursive reason, there may well be something higher than intelligence. Indeed, theism has always maintained that the Supreme Reason must be intuitive, in distinction from the discursiveness of human reason. The community and universality of intelligence, or of reason, does not consist in methods or processes, but in the rational contents. But this conception does not give us something above intelligence, but only above the human limitations of intelligence.

§ 28. The argument from the order of the universe sometimes takes a higher form in the claim that the intelligible universe not only demands intelligence as its cause, but is meaningless and non-existent except in reference to intelligence. This argument takes us into the depths of the theory of knowledge. The claim is made that the universe, as we conceive it, demonstrably demands intelligence as the condition of its existence. As light or sound, in the psychological sense, has neither meaning nor existence apart from the sensibility, so the universe itself is an absurdity and impossibility apart from conscious intelligence.

This argument does not commend itself to the natural man, nor even to the natural theist. Both alike are sure that the world of facts which they perceive is independent of their own intelligence, and of their neighbors' intelligence. This world did not begin when they first became aware of it, nor did it grow with their growing knowledge, nor will it vanish with their consciousness of it. This fact, which is admitted by all except some lively person who takes pleasure in airing conceits and paradoxes, is supposed by the natural man to show that the universe which exists apart from our intelligence exists apart from all intelligence. The natural theist, of course, would insist that the universe began in intelligence, but he would also insist that it now exists external to all intelligence. The atheist would claim that the universe is now, and always has been, external to intelligence. Both alike would be sure that the meaning of this externality is sun-clear, and that its reality is self-evident.

The question thus raised opens out into the debate between crude realism and rational idealism, and cannot be thoroughly discussed without a long metaphysical analysis of our fundamental notions. This cannot be undertaken here. We borrow, however, from metaphysics the conviction that relations can exist only in and for intelligence. But the universe as we know it is essentially a vast system of relations under the various categories of the intellect; and such a universe would have neither meaning nor existence apart from intelligence. It does not avail against this conclusion to say that, besides the relations, there are real things in relations; for these things themselves are defined and constituted by their relations, so that their existence apart from a constitutive intelligence becomes an absurdity. If, with Locke, we declare that relations are the work of the mind, and then attempt to find some unrelated reality in the object which can exist apart from mind, our quest is soon seen to be bootless and hopeless. In that case we should have to admit that the real in itself is unknowable, and that the real as known exists only in and for intelligence. But as this intelligence in and for which the universe exists is not ours, there must be a cosmic intelligence as its abiding condition, and in reference to which alone the affirmation of a universe has any meaning.

But this argument is highly abstract, and can never find favor except in speculative circles. It is valuable as showing theism, or a cosmic intelligence, to be a necessary implication of the essential structure of thought and knowledge. From this standpoint atheism would appear as the crude misunderstanding of a mind not yet in full possession of itself, but rather in hope-

less bondage to the senses and their spontaneous prejudices. We return to a more familiar
line of thought.

The Argument from Design.

The argument from order and intelligibility
is cosmic; it concerns the structure of the universe in itself, and in its relation to the knowing mind. But the laws of the system bear
no certain marks of purpose. If we ask how
they can be, we are referred to intelligence as
their explanation. If we ask what they are for,
the answer must be that we do not clearly see
that they are for anything. But this uncertainty vanishes when we come to the organic
world. Here we find activity according to a
plan, and results which are not merely products, but which have all the marks of purpose.
Here there are adjustments which look like contrivance, and combinations for manifest ends.
These facts are the data of the design argument.

These two arguments do not admit of sharp
separation; and perhaps a perfect knowledge
might find them one. Kant attempted to distinguish between the teleology of the organism
and the mere usableness of the inorganic world;

6

but this distinction cannot be rigorously maintained. Still, we find the most striking marks of design and contrivance in the organic world, and the reign of law, as such, does not imply purpose-like products. The reign of law is as absolute in the amorphous rock as in the crystal or in the living form. It is as absolute in the barren desert as in the fertile plain. But the results differ greatly in their power of suggesting intelligence. Finally, the argument from order has even been opposed to that from design, many fancying that the existence of fixed laws excludes the possibility of specific and detailed purposes. We may, then, consider the argument separately.

What has just been said may be restated in another form. The system of objective experience contains three factors which we are not at present able to connect by any logical deduction. The first and fundamental one is what is called the necessary truths of reason, or the system of rational categories. These are valid alike for the world of thought and the world of reality. They are the bond of union between the two, and found the possibility of knowledge. But there is no way of deducing the actual world from these categories of the reason. The second factor, the system of general laws, is indeed a specification under those categories, but is no necessary implication of them. And both the categories and the laws admit of manifold applications. The same set of laws could produce results altogether different from those of the actual system. Hence, neither the categories of the reason nor the general laws of the system explain the specific facts and combinations of the system. These, in turn, have to be admitted as opaque facts, or referred to purpose as their final ground. This is the third factor necessary for a complete comprehension of the system.

§ 29. The design argument has had varying fortunes. Verbal inaccuracies of statement have made room for floods of verbal criticism; and it has at times fallen into complete speculative disfavor. Nevertheless it will always be a great favorite with common-sense. Kant speaks of it with respect; and J. S. Mill regards it as the only theistic argument of any force whatever. It has been over and under estimated. It does not give us the full idea of God; but with the practical mind it will always be the main argument for the intelligence of the First Cause.

In studying this argument the following points are to be noted:

1. The argument is not: Design proves a designer. Here is design. Hence these things have had a designer. This would, formally at least, beg the question; for the very point is to know whether the minor premise be true. No one ever doubted that design implies a designer; but many have questioned whether the facts referred to design really justify this reference. The argument rather runs: Here are facts which have such marks of design and contrivance that we cannot explain them without referring them to purpose. The point is to solve the problem contained in the purpose-like adaptations and combinations found in the system; and the theist refers them to design or purpose as the only adequate solution. And whatever the verbal failings of the exposition may have been, this has always been the real meaning of the argument.

2. The design argument need assume nothing as to the way in which effects are produced. It claims only that adaptation in a complex product to an ideal end points to design somewhere.

3. Design is never causal. It is only an ideal conception, and demands some efficient cause, or system of efficient causes, for its realization. If the stomach is not to digest itself, there must be some provision for protecting it against the gastric juice. If ice is not to sink and freeze out life, there must be some molecular structure which shall make its bulk greater than that of an equal weight of water. If, then, efficient causes were commissioned to realize design, or, rather, if an ideal conception were impressed upon a system of efficient causes, so that the latter should work in accordance with the former, and realize the former, we should expect to see the products resulting with necessity from the nature of the agents at work. Watches produced by self-regulating machinery would point as certainly to intelligence as do watches produced by hand. In such a case we should have mechanical necessity itself working as the servant of purpose, and in forms prescribed by purpose.

4. Hence the study of efficient causes can never logically conflict with the belief in final causes. The former tells us how an effect has been brought about, and leaves us as free as

ever to believe that there was purpose in the doing. We can understand the grouping of efficient causes only by reference to final causes; and the final cause is realized only through the efficient cause.

5. Historically, the study of efficient causes has often tended to weaken the belief in final causes. This fact has several grounds:

A. The design argument has been supposed to teach an external making, and not an immanent guiding. Human designs are external to the material on which they are impressed; but this externality is in no way essential to the design. If the human maker, instead of adapting his plan to given material, could create his material outright and impress his plan upon its very being, the design would be quite as real and quite as apparent as it is now.

Under the influence of this fancy, the design argument has been much belabored. It has been called the carpenter theory — a phrase which, while missing the true nature of the argument, does most happily reveal the wooden nature of the criticism. But the argument itself is quite compatible with immanent design, with design legislated into the constitution of things, so that in their fixed order of unfolding they shall realize a predetermined plan or purpose.

B. The result of this blunder is a second, namely, the fancy that whatever can be explained by physical laws and agents is thereby rescued from the control of mind. Not even Kant is free from this confusion. In the " Critique of the Judgment " he suggests that the notion of purpose may have only a regulative value; and that possibly everything may have a mechanical explanation. Here he falls into the confusion of making design a cause among causes, and seems to think that we must not know how effects are produced if we are to believe them intended. Many have openly espoused this notion. The discovery that the stomach does not digest itself, because its walls secrete a fluid impervious to the gastric juice, has often been held to disprove the existence of purpose as the ground of the arrangement. This fancy, which recognizes purpose only where causation cannot be traced, had great influence in the late revival of atheism. Wherever natural laws could be traced, purpose was ruled out. This view first assumes that design is a cause, and then attributes self-sufficiency to the elements and laws of nature. If we knew nature to be at once self-sufficient and unintelligent, we might insist that the realms of mind and of nature are mutually exclusive. But in fact the system of things represents no self-sufficient existence, but only the way in which the world-ground proceeds. Whether there be any purpose in the proceeding can be known only by studying the outcome.

6. The chief ground for distinguishing between the system of law and specific design lies in what appears as the contrivances of nature. Here we have combinations of laws for the production of effects, which the laws taken singly do not involve. In organic forms especially we have a union of natural processes which, taken singly, would destroy the organism, but which together work for the maintenance of the whole. This class of facts has led many to think of design as something interjected into, or superinduced upon, a system essentially unrelated to it. But this fancy is reached by unlawful abstraction. It is indeed conceivable that there should be a system in which the elementary physical and chemical process should go on without any purpose-like products; but in the actual system

they are not thus resultless. When, then, we make the law into an abstract rule and separate it from its actual working and product, we merely analyze the complex reality into several factors for the convenience of our understanding; but which we need not regard as in any way representing the constituent factors from which the reality was produced. But this question goes too deeply into the question of the formal, and the objective signification of logical method, to be discussed to advantage here.

§ 30. The positive argument for design begins by showing that many processes in nature are determined by ends. The aim of the eye is vision, that of the ear is hearing, that of the lungs is the oxygenation of the blood, that of the manifold generative mechanisms is the reproduction of life. In all of these cases there is concurrence of many factors in a common result; and this result, towards which they all tend, is viewed as the final cause of their concurrence. Here, then, is action for an end. But an end, as such, cannot act except as a conception in the consciousness of some agent which wills that end. The end, as result, is effect, not cause. Hence activity for ends demands a preconceiving intelligence as its necessary implication or condition. Of course the standing answer to this argument is the claim that the apparent aims are not real ones; that they result from their antecedents by necessity and were never intended. Eyes were not made for seeing; but we have eyes, and see in consequence. The propagation of life was never purposed; but reproductive processes and mechanisms exist, and life is propagated. This view, in this naked form, has always scandalized the unsophisticated mind as a pettifogging affront to good sense.

There is no need to adduce instances of apparent purpose. They may be found in endless profusion in the various works on the subject. Besides, all admit that in the organic world the world - ground proceeds as if it had plans and purposes. The theistic conclusion is disputed on the following grounds:

1. The mechanism of nature explains the fact, and we need not go behind it.

2. The fact that the world-ground works *as if* it had plans does not prove that it has them.

3. There is no analogy between human activ-

ity and cosmic activity. We know that purpose
rules in human action, but we have no experience of world-making, and can conclude nothing
concerning cosmic action. The distance is too
great, and knowledge is too scant to allow any
inference.

All atheistic objections fall under some one
of these heads. We consider them in their
order.

§ 31. On the first point we observe that mechanism, and systems of necessity in general, can
never explain teleological problems. These can
find a final explanation only in a self-directing
intelligence. All other explanations are either
tautologies, or they implicitly abandon the problem. We have already pointed out that the
general laws of the system explain no specific
effect. Like the laws of motion, they apply to
all cases, but account for none. The specific
effect is always due to the peculiar circumstances under which the laws work. Hence, in
order to explain the effect, we must account for
not only the general laws, but also the special
circumstances which form the arbitrary con-
stants of the equation. But these cannot be

explained by any and every antecedent, but only by such as contain implicitly the effect. In that case we do not explain the peculiar nature of the effect, but only remove it one step further back. By the law of the sufficient reason, when we pass from effects to causes, we have to attribute them, not to any and every cause, but to causes which implicitly contain all the mystery and peculiarity of the effects. Thus the problem ever precedes us. We refer a to $-a$, and $-a$ is referred to $-2a$, and so on to $-na$. If $-na$ is given, then in the course of time a will appear; but at the farthest point, $-na$, we have a implicitly and necessarily given. In such a system we reach no resting-place and no true explanation. A given fact, a, is because $-a$ was; and $-a$ was because $-2a$ went before; and so on in endless regress. But as all later orders and collocations were implicit in $-na$, it follows that we deduce the present fact, a, from its antecedents by constructing our thought of those antecedents so as to contain the fact to be deduced. Of course it does not follow that a was given as a, but only in those antecedents which must lead to it; so that whoever could have read the system at any point in the past would

have seen *a* as a necessary implication. In a
system of necessity there can be no new departures, no interjection of new features, but
only an unfolding of the necessary implications.
If we make a cross-section of such a system at
any point, we find everything given either actually or potentially, and when an apparently new
fact appears, it is not something chanced upon,
but something which always must have been.
In such a scheme we do not come to the thought
of a beginning, but of a self-centred system, or
world - order, which rolls on forever, infolding
and unfolding all. This view might involve us
in sundry very grave metaphysical difficulties,
but we pass them over. The point to be noticed
is that this view does not solve, but only post-
pones, the teleological problem. If the facts
themselves call for explanation, just as much do
these hypothetical grounds demand it, for we
have simply carried the facts in principle into
them. But we conceal the fact from ourselves
by casting the shadow of necessity over the
whole, and this stifles further inquiry. Reference has already been made to the grotesque
inversion of reason which finds in the rational
order a ground for denying a basal reason; the

same thing meets us here. We construct our thought of the cosmic mechanism by an inverted teleology. The mechanism is simply teleology read backwards. But the notion of necessity so blinds us that the cosmic mechanism, which is but an incarnation of all cosmic products, is made the ground for denying purpose therein.

One reason for our failure to see that a necessary system must always implicitly contain all that comes out of it, is our failure to see that definite and specific effects can have only definite and specific causes. If anything could produce everything, there would be an end of all reasoning; for this proceeds according to the principle of the sufficient reason. But we trace the outlines of our system to some state of apparent homogeneity, say a nebula; and then conclude that any vague and formless matter must develop into fixed and definite purpose-like products. In our regress we forget the definite outcome, and thus we seem to reach the indefinite and meaningless. Then in our progress we remember the definite outcome again, and this passes for a deduction. Hence the nebular theory and that of natural selection have been often adduced as showing how, by a kind of mechanical necessity in a system of trial and rejection, purpose must result from non-purposive action. But here we fail entirely to be true to the principle of the sufficient reason, and mistake indefiniteness for the senses for indefiniteness for the reason. Indeed, there has always been at this point a curious oscillation in atheistic reasoning between chance and necessity. At times everything is absolutely determined; but when the design question is up, an element of indeterminateness appears. Some chaos, which contained nothing worth mentioning, or some raw beginnings of existence, which were so low as to make no demand for an intelligent cause, begins to shuffle into the argument. Being so abject, it excites no question or surprise. Being indeterminate, it does not seem to beg the question against teleology by implicitly assuming the problem; and then, by waving the magic wand of necessity, together with a happy forgetfulness of the laws of mental procedure, the nothing is transformed into an all-explaining something. We find the same fancy underlying the argument from the "conditions of existence," and the earlier whim that, as in infinite time all possible combinations must be

exhausted, the actual order must be hit upon.
The superficial and wooden nature of these notions need not be dwelt upon, as the very nature
of scientific method has rendered them obsolete.
They must be looked upon as survivals of a period when thought was groping blindly without
any knowledge of its own aims and methods.
In a necessary system there is no possible beyond the actual and its necessary implications.
All else is the impossible. There never was,
then, a period of indefiniteness out of which the
present order emerged by a happy chance. This
feature of all necessary systems vacates also the
theistic argument from probabilities. If there
ever had been a time when all was indefinite
and undetermined, it is highly improbable that
any rational order would have been hit upon.
But we cannot urge this against atheism, for
atheism which understands itself recognizes no
such period.

The mechanical explanation of a fact, then,
turns out to consist in assuming a cause or
causes of such a kind, and in such relations, that
they must produce that fact to the exclusion of
every other. But such an explanation is a pure
tautology, teleologically considered. It has to

frame the mechanism to fit the effects; and then the explanation of the effects is merely drawing out what was put in. The theist's point is missed entirely. He does not ask how effects are produced. He believes as well as the atheist that their efficient causes were adequate to their production. He contends only that an arrangement of efficient causes for the produc- tion of purpose-like effects points to mind and purpose as the ground of the arrangement. To this, which is the real point in dispute, there is only the well-worn answer that the arrangement is because it must be, and that there is no go- ing behind it. The argument from mechanism against teleology is simply a long irrelevance; for after we have referred everything to the mechanism, we find ourselves compelled to de- mand some unitary ground for the mechanism and its intelligible interaction.

§ 32. Throughout this argument against the- ism an assumption and an oversight are to be noticed. The assumption is that already re- ferred to, namely, that we directly know the proximate causes of phenomena, and know them to be material and unintelligent. As we know

7

the proximate causes, and find them daily explaining more and more, when we come to any new manifestation, instead of going outside of them for a cause apart, we need only enlarge our notion of these causes themselves. Be it far from us to tell what matter can or cannot do. How can we learn what it can do except by observing what it does? The illusion here is double. We assume (1) that we know causes in immediate perception, and (2) that their nature is at once mysterious and known. Mysterious, because we are going to determine it by studying what they do; and known, because the term matter carries with it certain implications which exclude intelligence. Thus, in great humility and self-renunciation, and with an air of extreme logical rigor, we build up a scheme of thought around a materialistic core, and fail to notice the transparent trick we are playing upon ourselves.

This assumption that the causes of phenomena are immediately given we have seen to be false. Causes are not seen. Their nature is a matter of speculative inference. Again, we have seen that even if we should find the proximate cause in material elements, we cannot regard them as independent, but must view them as dependent for all their laws and properties on an absolute world-ground. We cannot rest, then, in a system of things interacting according to mechanical laws, but must go behind the system to something which acts through it. The mechanical system is not ultimate and self-sufficient. It represents only the way in which the world-ground acts or determines things to act. If we ask why it thus acts, either we must regard it as a self-directing intellect, and find the reason in purpose, or we must affirm some opaque necessity in the world-ground itself, and say, It does what it does because it must.

The oversight referred to is the failure to see that man and mind are a part and outcome of the universe. The speculator, in curious self-forgetfulness, fixes his thought on the physical system and ignores himself. He assumes a monopoly of intellect in the universe, and forgets that this rare and lonely endowment must still have its roots in the universe. The problem then arises how to deduce the conscious from the unconscious, the intelligent from the non-intelligent, the purposive from the non-purposive, and freedom from necessity. But psychology shows the hopelessness of such a task. This insight has led to the modern device of a double - faced substance which, while stopping short of affirming an independent creative intelligence, does still insist upon intelligence as one of the original factors of the world-ground. The metaphysics of this view is somewhat open to suspicion, but it is correct in concluding that there is no way from non-intelligence to intelligence.

But if, on the other hand, we still insist on regarding the world-ground as mechanical, then we reach the same conclusion by a different road. For if everything is to be mechanically explained, then human life, thought, and action must be phases of the all-embracing necessity. But man can form purposes and determine himself accordingly. Hence it follows that in the department of human life, at least, the cosmic mechanism does form purposes and execute them. Here design actually appears as real and controlling. Hence, by the necessity of including man, we are forced to admit that the cosmic mechanism is not incompatible with purpose. But if it act purposely in the human realm, there is no theoretical objection to admitting that it acts purposely in the physical realm if the facts call for it. The only escape from this conclusion is to deny our consciousness that purpose rules at all in our mental life. But as long as this is allowed, the so-called cosmic mechanism must be viewed as one which can form plans and determine itself for their execution; that is, it must be what we mean by mind. The alternative, as we shall see, is to wreck knowledge in scepticism.

§ 33. The second general objection was, that the fact that the world-ground proceeds as if it had aims does not prove that it really has them. We have in this objection a relic of the ancient whim that atheism is sufficiently established by disputing theism. Let us allow that the fact that the world-ground proceeds as if it had purposes does not prove that it really has them; it is still clear that this fact is even further from proving that it does not have them.

To the general objection a first reply must be that all objective knowledge is based on an " as if." Not to refer to the scruples of idealism concerning the objects of perception, the whole of objective science is based on a certain truth of appearances. We do not know that there is an ether, but only that optical phenomena look as if there were. We do not know that atoms exist, but only that material phenomena look as if they did. We do not know that the fire rocks were ever molten, but only that they look as if they had been. We do not know that the sedimentary rocks were ever deposited from water, but only that they look so. That the present land was once under the sea is not known, but only a belief resting on certain appearances. But none of these conclusions could stand a minute if the principle of this objection were allowed. If the nature of things can produce the appearance of intelligence without its presence, it ought to be able to mimic igneous and aqueous action without the aid of either fire or water. If the hypothetical necessity of the system is competent to bring organic matter into a living form, it could certainly produce a fossil imitation at first hand; or, better, if the nature of things includes the production of living forms, it might also include the direct production of fossils. We cannot, then, conclude anything from fossil remains concerning the past history of our system; for this would be to conclude from an "as if;" and this is forbidden. If one should say, Well, how did they get there, anyhow? the answer would be that they are there because they must be there, and that no more can be said. If the questioner insisted, we should say that it is the height of absurdity to insist that things can be explained in only one way. Possibilities are infinite; and of these we can conceive only one; but it must be viewed as infinitely improbable that our little way of accounting for things is the way of the universe itself. It is, then, unspeakably rash to infer anything beyond what we see. It is curious that this argument should seem so profound, so judicious, so indicative of mental integrity when applied to theistic problems, and so unsatisfactory elsewhere. Without waiting to solve this psychological and logical puzzle, we point out that the theistic "as if" is as good as the scientific "as if." We cannot reject the one and retain the other.

§ 34. But we are not yet clear of the "as if." In general we know what a force is only by observing what it does. This is especially the case with mind, which is never seen in itself, but only in its effects. And this is true not only of the divine mind, but of the human mind as well. A mistake which flows directly from our general bondage to the senses leads us to fancy that we see our neighbors' minds; and it has generally been argued against theism that we see mind in man, but none in nature. This claim the rudiments of psychology dispel. We know that our fellow-beings have minds only because they act as if they had; that is, because their action shows order and purpose. In short, the argument for objective intelligence is the same whether for man, animals, or God. But no one will claim that the system of things shows less order and purpose than human action. If, then, we deny mind in nature because we have only an " as if" to reason from, we must deny it also in man; for an " as if" is all we have here. And yet we are wonderfully ready to find objective intelligence, if only it is not referred to God. The scantiest marks prove the presence of intellect in man and brute, or in human and brute action; but nothing proves intelligence back of nature. The ground of this queer logic must be sought in a profound study of the philosophy of prejudice and confusion.

The point just dwelt upon deserves further notice. The belief in personal co-existence has never been questioned by the extremest idealists; and we find it in full strength in our earliest years. To explain this fact some have called it an instinct, while others have preferred the more distinguished title of an intuition. And there are the best of reasons why this belief should be made an absolute certainty in advance of all argument, and even against it. The certainty of personal co-existence constitutes the chief condition of a moral activity; and if it were in any way weakened, the most hideous results might follow. Nevertheless, the logical ground of the belief consists entirely in the fact that our neighbors act as if they were intelligent. And upon reflection one must confess that the activities from which we infer intelligence are not very striking, but rather such as the organism might well execute of itself. And in all of these cases, even in the use of speech, if we should study the effect, which is always some form of physical movement, we should doubtless find a physical explanation. In the case of speech we should find no thought in the effect; that would be an addition of our own.

We have simply vibrating air, which can be traced to vibrating membranes, which in turn are set in motion by currents of air; and these are forced along by the contraction of muscles producing a contraction of the thorax. If we care to pursue it further we soon lose ourselves in the mystery of nervous currents, and the subject escapes us. Nowhere in the series do we come in sight of a mind. We have, to be sure, an outcome which happens to be intelligible; but the atheist has instructed us that intelligibility in the outcome is far enough from proving an intelligent cause. Besides, the outcome, so far as we can trace it, has a purely mechanical explanation, and need be referred to no mind. It would be a highly suspicious circumstance and a grave infraction of the law of continuity to conclude that a series which is physical as far as we can trace it, becomes something else where we cannot trace it. It has been customary to say that we know that watches are designed, but not that eyes are designed. This is a mistake. In the case of a watchmaker we do not see the workman any more than in the case of the eye. We see only a physical organism in complex interaction with surrounding matter, and we see that the work goes on as if for an end; but we see nothing more. The living, thinking workman is an inference from an "as if." But in nature, too, the work goes on as if for an end; and the "as-ifness" is at least as marked as in the former case. If, then, watches point to an unseen workman who knows what he is doing, nature also points to an unseen workman who knows what he is doing. Any doubt of the one must extend to the other. But if we may be practically sure of our neighbors' intelligence, and that because they act intelligently, we may be sure that the world-ground is intelligent for the same reason.

§ 35. But we must go a step further. The last paragraph showed that the same argument which discredits mind in nature throws equal doubt upon mind in man. But further reflection shows that if there be no controlling mind in nature there can be no controlling mind in man. For if the basal power is blind and necessary, all that depends upon it is necessitated also. In that case all unfolding is driven from behind, and nothing is led from before. Thought and feeling also come within this necessary un-

folding.   As such they are products, not causes.
The basal necessity controls them in every respect, yet without being in any sense determined
by them.   Thought as thought counts for nothing.   The line of power is through the mechanical antecedents which condition thought, and
not through the thought itself.   Hence any
fancy of self-control we may have must be dismissed as delusive.   Human life and history,
then, express no mind or purpose, but only the
process of the all-embracing necessity. Thought
and purpose may have been there as subjective
states; but they must be put outside of the
dynamic sequence of events, and be made a kind
of halo which, as a shadow, attends without af-
fecting the cosmic movement.   Indeed, so far
from solving, thought rather complicates the
problem.   It offers no guidance, and is so much
more to be accounted for.   The basal necessity
has not only to produce the physical movements
and groupings which we mistakenly ascribe to
intelligence, but it has also to produce the illusion of conscious thought and self-control. This
extremely difficult and delicate task is escaped
by denying the human mind outright; and this
is not difficult, as we affirm objective mind only

from the conviction that its guidance is necessary. When this conviction is lacking, there is no ground for affirming objective thought.

The claim, then, that we know watches are designed, but do not know that eyes are designed, appears to be doubly untenable. First, we have the same proof that eyes are designed that we have that watches are designed; and second, if eyes are not designed, then watches are not designed. Both alike result from necessity, and if any thought attends the process, it does not affect it.

The truth is, the design argument derives its force from the consciousness of our own free effort. We find that combinations for ends arise in our experience only as they first exist in conception, and are then made the norms of our action. And wherever we find combination apparently for ends, we at once supply the pre-existent conception and the self-determination which experience has shown to be its invariable condition. We have already seen that in a system of necessity, teleological questions can never be answered; it is further plain that in such a system they could never logically arise. Such questions imply that things might have been otherwise, and hence involve a denial of the complete determination of all existence. When such determination is consciously affirmed, to ask why anything is as it is, is like asking why a straight line is the shortest distance between two points. Spinoza is the only leading necessitarian who has clearly seen the opposition between necessity and teleology. Most necessitarians have oscillated between this insight and attempts at mechanical explanation which should satisfy the teleological craving. This inconsequence would seem to show that the cosmic necessity itself is somewhat illogical.

§ 36. The third general objection, that the difference between human action and cosmic action is too great to allow any conclusion from one to the other, is only a large way of saying nothing. Theism argues from intelligible effects to an intelligent cause. The rational and intelligible work is referred to intelligence and reason. The suggestion that we have a knowledge in objective human action which we do not have in cosmic action is mistaken. The further demurrer that while intelligibility in human action points to intelligence, intelligibility in cosmic action does not point to intelligence, is an act of caprice, not of reason. If it be further suggested that there may be untold transcendental possibilities any one of which might produce the effects, this is only to return to the unreason of abandoning reason in order to revel in inarticulate imaginings, none of which can be constructed in thought.

As a result of all these considerations we hold that the design argument, when the unity of the world-ground is given, proves far more conclusively the existence of mind in nature than it does the existence of mind in man. The two stand or fall together.

Argument from the Theory of Knowledge

§ 37. We have already dwelt upon the rational structure of the universe involved in the assumed possibility of knowledge, and also upon the impossibility of comprehending this structure without assuming it to be founded in a rational being who is its author. We propose now to consider the bearings of atheism upon the problem of knowledge.

No theory can be allowed to commit suicide; and when a theory is shown to be suicidal it is self-condemned. In particular no theory can be allowed which would overturn reason itself. The trustworthiness of reason is the presupposition of all speculation; and when a theory conflicts with this, it must be rejected. One could not accept it without admitting that all theories are doubtful, this one among the rest. This is the case with atheism, and with all systems of necessity.

§ 38. Beliefs can be viewed in two ways: as produced by causes, or as deduced from grounds. That is, beliefs may be merely mental events due to certain psychological antecedents, and they may be logical convictions which rest on logical grounds. The distinction of rational from irrational beliefs is that the former have grounds which justify them, while the latter are only effects in us, deposits of habit, prejudice, tradition, caprice, etc. They have their sufficient psychological causes, but have no justifying rational grounds. Now every system of necessity cancels this distinction. It gives us causes, but removes the grounds, of belief. The proof is as follows:

In every mechanical doctrine of mind there

are no mental acts, but only psychological occurrences. Even the drawing of a conclusion is not an act of the mind, but an occurrence in the mind. The conclusion is not justified by its antecedent reasons, but is coerced by its psychological antecedents. If we deny the substantiality of mind, the conclusion is only the mental symbol of a certain state of the physical mechanism. If we allow the mind to be real, but subject to necessity, then the conclusion is but the resultant of the preceding mental states. In both cases we must replace the free, self-centred activity of reason by a physical or mental mechanism which determines all our ideas and their conjunctions. This determination takes on in consciousness the appearance of reflection, reasoning, concluding, etc., but these are only the illusive symbols in consciousness of a mechanical process below it. Nothing, then, depends on reason, but only on the physical or mental states; and these, for all we know, might become anything whatever with the result of changing the conclusion to any other whatever. But this view is the extreme of scepticism. Beliefs sink into effects; and one is as good as another while it lasts. The coming or going of

8

a belief does not depend upon its rationality, but only on the relative strength of the corresponding antecedents. But this strength is a fact, not a truth. When a given element displaces another in a chemical compound, it is not truer than that other, but stronger. So when a psychical element displaces another in a mental combination, not truth, but strength, is in question. On the plane of cause and effect, truth and error are meaningless distinctions. Proper rationality is possible only to freedom; and here truth and error first acquire significance. The rational mind must not be controlled by its states, but must control them. It must be able to stand apart from its ideas and test them. It must be able to resist the influence of habit and association, and to undo the irrational conjunctions of custom. It must also be able to think twice, and to reserve its conclusions until the inner order of reason has been reached. Unless it can do this, all beliefs sink into effects, and the distinction of rational and irrational, of truth and error, vanishes.

We reach the same conclusion from another standpoint. No system of necessity has any standard of distinction between truth and error.

If all beliefs are not true, and as contradictory they cannot be, it follows that error is a fact. But how can error be admitted without cancelling truth? On the one hand, we must admit that our faculties are made for truth, and that we cannot by volition change truth. On the other, we cannot allow that we are shut up by necessity to error, as then our faculties would be essentially untrustworthy. This difficulty can be resolved only in the notion of freedom. If we have faculties which are truthful, but which may be carelessly used or wilfully misused, we can explain error without compromising truth; but not otherwise. If truth and error be alike necessary, there is no standard of truth left. If we make the majority the standard, what shall assure us that the majority is right? And who knows that the majority will always hold the same views? Opinions have changed in the past, why not in the future. There is no rational standard left, and no power to use it if there were. We cannot determine our thoughts; they come and go as the independent necessity determines. If there were any reason left, the only conclusion it could draw would be that knowledge is utterly impossible, and that its place must be swallowed up by an overwhelming scepticism.

The bearing of this upon theism is plain. There can be no rationality, and hence no knowledge, upon any system of necessity. Atheism is such a system, and hence is suicidal. It must flout consciousness, discredit reason, and end by dragging the whole structure of thought and life down into hopeless ruin. Rationality demands freedom in the finite knower; and this, in turn, is incompatible with necessity in the world-ground. This freedom does not, indeed, imply the power on the part of the mind to coerce its conclusions, but only to rule itself according to preconceived standards. Pure arbitrariness and pure necessity are alike incompatible with reason. There must be a law of reason in the mind with which volition cannot tamper; and there must also be the power to determine ourselves accordingly. Neither can dispense with the other. The law of reason in us does not compel obedience, else error would be impossible. Rationality is reached only as the mind accepts the law and determines itself accordingly.

We conclude, then, from the total argument

that if the trustworthiness of reason is to be maintained, it can be only on a theistic basis; and since this trustworthiness is the presupposition of all science and philosophy, we must say that God, as free and intelligent, is the postulate of both science and philosophy. If these are possible, it can be only on a theistic basis.

§ 39. A not entirely irrelevant aside may be allowed on the two factors of freedom and necessity. Complete determination is necessity, and overturns reason. Complete indetermination, if possible, would be pure chance, and would equally overturn reason. Freedom, therefore, has to assume a certain element of uniformity in order to acquire any value or meaning; and necessity has to assume a factor of freedom. Within the human mind, the element of uniformity is found in the mental nature and laws of thought and judgment; and the element of freedom lies in our power to rule ourselves in accordance with those laws. To deny either element is fatal. In the cosmos these two factors can be adjusted to the demands of thought only in the notion of a rational work depending upon a free intelligence. The work is determined throughout according to principles of reason, and thus admits of being rationally construed. But back of the work is the free worker as its ground and cause. Mental unsteadiness is common at this point. The understanding can grasp only the determined, and hence it is tempted to posit everything as absolutely determined. This lust of understanding must be overcome by the insight that freedom is a condition of the understanding itself, and that in a system of pure necessity nothing whatever can be understood.

§ 40. Thus far we have sought to show that the facts of human intelligence and of cosmic law and order demand intelligence in the world-ground as their only sufficient explanation. This line of argument may be brought to a close by assuming the theistic and atheistic hypotheses respectively, and inquiring how the facts illustrate and support them. This is a recognized form of logical procedure in dealing with hypotheses. We may either study the facts and deduce the hypothesis, or we may form the hypothesis and test it by the facts. In the former case all facts are ruled out which do not distinctly demand the hypothesis; in the latter case all the facts are included which do not positively oppose the hypothesis. The best result is reached by combining the two. By the first method the hypothesis acquires a positive support, and by the second it may be greatly extended.

Let us suppose, then, that the universe is founded in intelligence. We find the facts agreeing thereto. There is a rational work, according to rational methods, for intelligible ends. To be sure our knowledge is limited, but, so far as we can understand, we find the marks of transcendent wisdom. In such a case it is not hard to believe that a larger knowledge would make this more and more apparent; just as we believe that a deeper insight would reveal the reign of law in realms apparently lawless.

Let us next make the opposite assumption that the universe is founded in non-intelligence. Now nothing is what we should expect. We find an irrational power doing a rational work. An unconscious power produces consciousness. Non-intelligence produces intelligence. Necessity produces freedom. The non-purposive works apparently for purpose. The unexpected meets us at every turn. The facts appear in irreconcilable and growing hostility to the hypothesis.

There is no need to pursue these considerations. It seems plain (1) that the belief in a free and intelligent ground of things is as well founded as any objective belief whatever, and (2) that this belief is one which enters so intimately into our mental life that philosophy and science, and even rationality itself stand or fall with it. On all these accounts we hold that the universe is founded in intelligence. The conception of necessary mechanical agency as first and fundamental leads to no true insight, and ends in total mental collapse. Self-directing rational agency is the only principle that gives any light, or that can be made basal without immediate self-stultification. Atheism and necessity should be declared mental outlaws, and a perpetual rational injunction should be placed upon their appearance in the intellectual world. The dreary farce of appealing to reason in support of principles which destroy reason ought sometime to come to an end. If one should deny reason, and forever after held his peace, his position would be consistent; but whoever will insist on appealing to reason should in self-respect and good faith debar himself from all theories which deny it.   Failure to do so is a procedure on the level of a solipsist who, while pretending to doubt his neighbor's existence, should nevertheless apply to him for arguments to prove that existence.   Many bright and acute things might be said, but the farce would be apparent.

CHAPTER III.

THE WORLD-GROUND AS PERSONAL.

§ 41. The direct argument for the intelligence of the world-ground is conclusive; and unless counter-argument can be found the conclusion must be allowed to stand. But there is a very general agreement among speculators that such argument exists, and of such force withal as greatly to weaken, if not to overthrow, the theistic conclusion. In particular the objection is made that personality, and hence intelligence, cannot be attributed to an absolute and infinite being, as these notions are distinctly incompatible. While, then, we are shut up on the one side to the belief in an intelligent, and hence personal, world-ground, we are shut out on the other by the contradictory character of the conception. This might be called the antinomy of the theistic argument.

§ 42. Before proceeding to the argument an

attempt at mediation must be noticed. Many have held to the intelligence and rationality of the world-ground who yet have denied its personality. This view has found expression in many poetical, or rather imaginative, utterances of pantheism. These have some attraction for the fancy, but most of them offer nothing to the intellect. Along with an astonishing fecundity of phrases there has been a still more astonishing barrenness of thought.

Some have proposed to conceive 'the world-ground as a double-faced substance; on the one side extension and form, and on the other side life and reason. These two sides constitute the reality of the outer and inner worlds respectively. This conception finds expression in Spinoza, and in many modern monistic systems. It is based upon the antiquated notion of substance as extended stuff, and upon the fictitious abstraction of thought. No one has ever succeeded in forming any conception of what a double-faced substance might mean. The imagination, indeed, masters the problem at once. A thing is conceived with two sides, and one side is called thought; but this performance is not finally satisfactory. Again the relation of the two faces, the physical and the mental, is a problem which has not received its solution. If the two go along in complete independence, there is nothing in the physical world on the one hand to suggest thought; and there is nothing in thought on the other hand to suggest the physical world. An outright denial of the latter would be the immediate result. In short, this doctrine must retreat into the affirmation of a transcendental something above thought and extension; and this is only the well-known phrase to which there is no corresponding thought.

Insight into the emptiness of the doctrine of a transcendental X, and into the impossibility of founding the system in simple material existence, has led many to give another form to their non-theistic views. The world-ground has been called pure will, unconscious intelligence, impersonal reason, impersonal spirit, universal life, etc. But these too are empty phrases, obtained by unlawful abstraction. For Schopenhauer the world-ground is pure will without intellect or personality. But pure will is nothing. Will itself, except as a function of a conscious and intelligent spirit, has no meaning. When the conscious perception of ends and the conscious determination of self according to those ends are dropped, there is nothing remaining that deserves to be called will. We may befog ourselves with words, but the conception of a blind and necessary force is all that remains.

Unconscious intelligence is an oft-recurring notion in speculation. The *anima mundi* of the Platonic physics and the plastic principle of Cudworth are examples. This conception has often found a place in theistic systems from a desire, first, to recognize something higher than corpuscular mechanics in the world of life, and, second, to free God from the onerous duty of administering the details of the universe. Hartmann has extended this notion to the world-ground itself. Against atheism he affirms its intelligence; against theism he maintains its unconsciousness. But in the phrase, unconscious intelligence, the adjective devours the noun in its attempt to agree with it, and the noun agrees so ill with the adjective as to destroy it altogether. Only one clear thought can be joined to this phrase, namely, that of blind forces, which are not intelligent at all, but which nevertheless work to produce intelligible results.

The same is true of the phrase, impersonal reason.   Reason itself is a pure abstraction which
is realized only in conscious spirits; and when
we abstract from these all that constitutes them
conscious persons there is nothing intelligible
left.   By impersonal reason also we could only
mean a blind force which is not reason, but
which is adjusted to the production of rational
results.   In this sense any machine has impersonal reason.

Instinct is the standing illustration of unconscious intelligence and impersonal reason; but
it fails to illustrate.   For if instinctive acts are
not performed with purpose and consciousness,
they are not outcomes of intelligence at all, but
of a mechanical necessity which mimics intelligence.   This necessity may lie in the constitution of the agent, or in its physical structure, or
in the relations of both to surroundings; but in
any case there is no intelligence in play, unless
it be the intelligence of the Creator upon which
the necessity itself depends.   To a mind which
has not developed enough to see that all thinking must be in intelligible terms, this must seem
horribly dogmatic.   Who can tell what the awful Possible may contain?   Who, indeed?   But

all who are developed far enough to see that thought is impossible without meanings, know that our affair is not with the awful Possible, but with the much humbler problem of finding that conception of the world-ground which will make the universe most intelligible to us. And for this sane state of mind, intelligence and reason are such only as they are guided by ends; and a guidance by ends means nothing except as those ends are present in consciousness as ideal aims. When this is not the case we have neither reason nor intelligence, but only necessary agency which may mimic rational activity.

The meaning of the previous doctrines may be summed up in the notion of an impersonal spirit, which is the ground of all existence, and which comes to consciousness only in finite spirits. But this, too, is more easily said than understood. In fact it is simply atheism under another name. What the atheist calls persistent force or the fundamental reality, is here called impersonal spirit; but the meaning is in both cases the same. Both alike understand by the terms that blind and necessary reality which underlies all phenomena, and which, in its necessary on-going, brings to life and death. But

as the new phrase implies the old thing we need
not consider it further. We conclude that if
the world-ground be intelligent and rational, it
must also be conscious and personal.

§ 43. The world-ground must be absolute and
infinite, and these attributes are incompatible
with consciousness and personality. In considering this objection we first remark that personality is not to be confounded with corporeality,
or with form of any sort. This confusion underlies the traditional criticism, dating back to
Xenophanes, that speculating cattle would infer
a God like themselves. Oxen, buffaloes, and
even watches have been used to illustrate this
profound objection. But if a speculative watch
should conclude, not to springs, levers, and es-
capements, but to intelligence in its maker, it
would not seem to be very far astray. By personality, then, we mean only self-knowledge and
self-control. Where these are present we have
personal being; where they are absent the being
is impersonal. Now that the ability to know
itself and what it is doing should be denied to
the ground and source of all power and knowledge, is a denial so amazing as to require the

best reasons to support it. It is really one of the most extraordinary inversions in speculation, and a striking example of the havoc which can be wrought by using words without attending to their meaning.

And first it is said that all consciousness involves the distinction of subject and object, and hence is impossible to an isolated and single being. It is, then, incompatible with both the infinity of the world-ground and with its singleness. As infinite, it can have nothing beyond itself, and as only it can have no object. But this claim mistakes a mental form for an ontological distinction. The object in all consciousness is always only our presentations, and not something ontologically diverse from the mind itself. These presentations may stand for things, but consciousness extends only to the presentations. In self-consciousness this is manifestly the case. Here consciousness is a consciousness of our states, thoughts, etc., as our own. The Infinite, then, need not have something other than himself as his object, but may find the object in his own activities, cosmic or otherwise.

This fact contains the answer to another form of objection. The ego and non-ego are said to

9

be two correlative notions, neither of which has any meaning apart from the other. Hence the conception of the self can arise only as the conception of the not-self arises with it; and hence, again, self-consciousness is possible only for finite beings who are limited by a not-self.

It is only with effort that one can believe the first part of this claim to be seriously made. Two notions whose meaning consists in denying each other are pure negations without any positive content. Thus, A is not-B, and B is not-A; and hence A is not-not-A, and B is not-not-B. We end where we began. To make any sense one of the notions must have a positive meaning independent of the other. And in the case of ego and the non-ego, it is plain which is the positive notion. The ego is the immediately experienced self, and the non-ego is originally only the sum of mental presentations, or that which the ego sets over against itself in consciousness as its object. Secondarily, the non-ego comes to mean whatever is excluded from the conscious self. Each person sets all his objects, whether persons or things, over against himself, and they constitute the non-ego for him. By overlooking this ambiguity, some speculators have proved a rich variety of truths. Idealism has been confounded by pointing out that consciousness demands an object as well as a subject, and the reality of matter has been solidly established. Consciousness demands a non-ego; and is not matter pre-eminently a non-ego!

The further claim that the conception of self can arise only as the conception of a not-self accompanies it, is but a repetition of the preceding objection concerning the ego and non-ego. Consciousness does involve the co-existence of these conceptions as the form under which consciousness arises, but not as things ontologically diverse. The distinction of subject and object, on which consciousness depends, is only a mental function, and not an ontological distinction. The possibility of personality or self-consciousness in no way depends on the existence of a substantial not-self, but only on the ability of the subject to grasp its states, thoughts, etc., as its own. It is, indeed, true that our consciousness begins, and that it is conditioned by the activity of something not ourselves; but it does not lie in the notion of consciousness that it must begin, or that it must be aroused from without. An eternal, unbegun self is as possible as an eternal, unbegun not-self. Eternal consciousness is no more difficult than eternal unconsciousness; and withal, if unconsciousness had ever been absolute there is no way of reaching consciousness. In addition, all the sceptical difficulties which attend that view crowd upon us. Hence to the question, What is the object of the Infinite's consciousness? the answer is, The Infinite himself, his thoughts, states, etc. To the question, When did this consciousness begin? the answer is, Never. To the question, On what does this consciousness depend? the answer is, On the Infinite's own power to know.

§ 44. On all these accounts we regard the objections to the personality of the world-ground as resting on a very superficial psychology. So far as they are not verbal, they arise from taking the limitations of human consciousness as essential to consciousness in general. In fact we must reverse the common speculative dogma on this point, and declare that proper personality is possible only to the Absolute. The very objections urged against the personality of the

Absolute show the incompleteness of human personality. Thus it is said, truly enough, that we are conditioned by something not ourselves. The outer world is an important factor in our mental life. It controls us far more than we do it. But this is a limitation of our personality rather than its source. Our personality would be heightened rather than diminished, if we were self-determinant in this respect. Again, in our inner life we find similar limitations. We cannot always control our ideas. They often seem to be occurrences in us rather than our own doing. The past vanishes beyond recall; and often in the present we are more passive than active. But these, also, are limitations of our personality. We should be much more truly persons if we were absolutely determinant of all our states. But we have seen that all finite things have the ground of their existence, not in themselves, but in the Infinite, and that they owe their peculiar nature to their mutual relations and to the plan of the whole. Hence, in the finite consciousness, there will always be a foreign element, an external compulsion, a passivity as well as activity, a dependence on something not ourselves, and a corresponding subjection. Hence in us personality will always be incomplete. The absolute knowledge and self-possession which are necessary to perfect personality can be found only in the absolute and infinite being upon whom all things depend. In his pure self-determination and perfect self-possession only do we find the conditions of complete personality; and of this our finite personality can never be more than the feeblest and faintest image.

§ 45. In leaving this subject a word must be said about a series of objections from the agnostics. These hold that the world-ground is no object of thought whatever, and hence cannot be thought of as personal or impersonal, as intelligent or non-intelligent. The reason is found in the mutual contradictions alleged to exist between the necessary attributes of the fundamental being. Thus we must regard it as self-centred, and hence absolute; as unlimited by anything beyond itself, and hence infinite, and as world-ground, that is, as first cause. But while we are shut up by thought to these admissions, we are equally shut out from them by their mutual contradiction. Thus the first cause, as such, exists only in relation to the effect. If it had no effect, it would not be cause. Hence the first cause is necessarily related to its effect; and hence it cannot be absolute; for the absolute exists out of all relations. The absolute cannot be a cause, and a cause cannot be absolute. Nor can we help ourselves by the idea of time, as if the world-ground first existed as absolute, and then became a cause; for the other notion of the infinite bars our way. That which passes into new modes of existence either surpasses or sinks below itself, and in either case cannot be infinite, for the infinite must always comprise all possible modes of existence. Hence we have in these necessary attributes a disheartening, and even sickening, contradiction which shatters all our pretended knowledge.

If this argument had not passed for important, we should refer to it only with expressions of apology. In itself it is mainly a play on words. Etymologically the above meanings may be tortured out of the terms. The infinite may be taken as the quantitative all; the absolute may be taken as the unrelated; and then the conclusions follow. The infinite as quantitative all must, of course, be all-embracing. Outside of the all there can be nothing; and if the all must comprehend all possible modes of existence at all times, it cannot change; and the universe is brought to the rigid monotony of the Eleatics. It is equally easy to show that the absolute cannot be related when we define it as the unrelated. But all this wisdom disappears when we remember the philosophical meaning of the terms. Both absolute and infinite mean only the independent ground of things. Relative existence is that which exists only in relation to other things. Both the ground and form of its existence are bound up in its relations. Such relations are restrictions, and imply dependence. But absoluteness denies this restriction and dependence. The absolute may exist in relations, provided those relations are freely posited by itself, and are not forced upon it from without. The infinite, again, is not the quantitative all. This " all " is purely a mental product which represents nothing apart from our thought. The world-ground is called infinite, because it is believed to be the independent source of the finite and its limitations, yet without being bound by them except in the sense of logical consistency. But in this sense the notions of the absolute and infinite are so far from incompatible that they mutually imply each other, or are but different aspects of the same thing. The infinite would not be infinite if it were not absolute; and neither infinite nor absolute would be anything if it were not a cause.

A final affectation must be mentioned. The claim has been set up that to attribute design of any kind to God is a limitation. This claim rests upon the fact that we often use design as equivalent to contrivance, and contrivance, in turn, has various meanings. It may be the equivalent of design, or the adaptation of parts; and it may be a makeshift for avoiding difficulties, or a combination of things or processes for doing indirectly what our power or skill could not directly accomplish. Here, then, is a fine opportunity for critical acumen, and it has not been overlooked. We have but to take contrivance as implying puzzle-headedness or inadequacy to see that it cannot be affirmed of God. When, in addition, we discreetly overlook the fact that in theism it means only the rational connection of many factors with reference to an ideal end, unless the audience be too critical, we may at once proclaim the incompatibility of design with the absoluteness of the world-ground. Such an antinomy could not fail to prove a veritable metaphysical Medusa to theistic faith.

The history of philosophy abounds in grotesque and whimsical misunderstandings; but of these none are more extraordinary than the artificial and gratuitous difficulties which have been raised over the question of the divine personality.

CHAPTER IV.

THE METAPHYSICAL ATTRIBUTES OF THE WORLD-GROUND.

§ 46. OUR speculative conception of the world-ground begins to approximate to the religious conception of God. A great variety of influences, instinctive, speculative, and ethical, have led the human mind to build up the conception of a personal and intelligent God; and this view, when criticised, not only proves able to maintain itself, but also appears as a demand and implication of reason itself. But the race has not contented itself with this bare affirmation, but, by an intellectual labor extending over centuries, it has sought to determine more closely the content of its theistic thought. These determinations fall into two classes, metaphysical and ethical. The former aim to tell what God is by virtue of his position as first cause, and the second relate to his character. Or the former refer to the divine nature, the latter to the divine will. Beyond this distinction, the various classifications of the divine attributes in which dogmatic theology abounds have no significance for either speculative or religious thought. We pass now to consider the leading metaphysical attributes as belonging to the world-ground. The result will be to show a still closer approximation of religious and speculative thought. We begin also to use the terms, God and world-ground, as interchangeable.

§ 47. The unity of the world-ground is the first of these metaphysical attributes; and the necessity of its affirmation is found in a study of interaction. But necessary as it is, its meaning is not always clearly grasped. We need, then, to inquire of metaphysics what is meant by the unity of being in general.

In affirming unity of a thing the primal aim is to deny composition and divisibility. A compound is not a thing, but an aggregate. The reality is the component factors. The thought of a compound is impossible without the assumption of units; and if these are compounds we must assume other units; and so on until we come to ultimate and uncompounded units.

These are the true realities. Hence, the divisible is never a proper thing, but a sum or a crowd. When, then, we say that a thing is a unit, we mean first of all that it is not compounded, and does not admit of division. Hence the doctrine of the unity of the world-ground is first of all a denial of composition and divisibility.

Unity has been taken to mean simplicity, or the opposite of complexity and variety. Herbart especially has identified them, and has declared that unity of the subject is incompatible with plurality of attributes. The same view has often appeared in treating of the divine unity. This has been conceived as pure simplicity; and thus the divine being has been reduced to a rigid and lifeless stare. This view brings thought to a standstill; for the one, conceived as pure simplicity, leads to nothing and explains nothing. It contains no ground of differentiation and progress. So, then, there is a very general agreement that the unity of the world-ground must contain some provision for manifoldness and complexity.

The history of thought shows a curious uncertainty at this point. On the one hand, there has been a universal demand for unity with a very general failure to reach it. And on the other hand, if the unity has been reached, there has been quite as general an inability to make any use of it. This is a necessary result of thinking only under mechanical conditions. In such thinking, when we begin with a plurality, we never escape it, for mechanical necessity cannot differentiate itself. If we trace the plurality to some one being, we are forced to carry the plurality implicitly into the unity, as there is no way of mechanically deducing plurality from unity. But in that case, though we confidently talk about unity, we are quite unable to tell in what the unity of such a being consists. If, on the other hand, we assume the unity, we are unable to take one step towards plurality. The all-embracing unity refuses to differentiate or to move at all.

This puzzle can be solved only by leaving the mechanical realm for that of free intellect. The free and conscious self is the only real unity of which we have any knowledge, and reflection shows that it is the only thing which can be a true unity. All other unities are formal, and have only a mental existence. But free intelligence, by its originating activity, can posit plurality distinct from its own unity, and by its self-consciousness, can maintain its unity and identity over against the changing plurality. Here the one is manifold without being many. Here unity gives birth to plurality without destroying itself. Here the identical changes and yet abides. But this perennial wonder is possible only on the plane of free and self-conscious intelligence. For mechanical thinking the problem admits only of verbal solutions.

So much for the metaphysics of unity. Probably, however, the thought most generally connected with the divine unity is not so much that God is one as that God is only. Hence the doctrine has been always monotheism, and not henotheism. The historic influences which have led to this monotheistic faith are manifold; and its speculative necessity is stringent. The thought of many gods, each of which should live in a world by himself, or rather, in a universe of his own, is a pure fancy due to the abstracting and hypostasizing tendency of the mind. If they should meet and interact in a common universe they would necessarily become finite and conditioned beings in mutual interaction, and hence not independent and self-existent. The discussion of the unity of the world-ground has shown that all things which are bound up in a scheme of interaction must have their existence in some one being on which they depend. This being founds the system, and all that is in the system flows from it. But we are able to form general notions, and then to conceive an indefinite number of members of the class. We do the same with the universe and the fundamental being. We form the notions, and then fancy that there may be other universes and other fundamental realities. But plainly such fancies are mental fictions. The actual universe, whereby we mean the total system of the finite, must be referred to the one world-ground. The imaginary systems need nothing for their explanation beyond the somewhat unclear mind that forms them and mistakes them for realities. If one should ask how we know that there may not be something entirely independent of our system and totally unrelated to it, the answer would be that our business is with the actual universe, and does not include the disproof of chimeras. This only may be allowed. If by universe we mean the system of sense-perceptions in an idealistic sense, the one world-ground may maintain a series of such systems.   In this sense a number of universes would be possible, but the unity and singleness of the fundamental reality would still be necessary.

This fact has often been disregarded in speculation.   Not a few have been pleased to regard space, time, and God as mutually independent existences, or rather to make space and time into pre-existent necessities to which God himself must submit.   How these independent and unrelated existences could be brought into mutual relations is a problem left unsolved.

The unity of the world-ground means, then, not only that it is uncompounded, indivisible, and without distinction of parts, but also that there is but one such fundamental existence.

§ 48. A second attribute is that of unchangeability.   This attribute has often been verbally interpreted with the result of reducing existence to a fixed rigidity from which all life and movement are excluded.   The Eleatics made being one and changeless, and were then utterly unable to account for the world of plurality and change.   A similar mistake often appears in speculative theology.   It has sometimes so em-

10

phasized the unchangeability as to lose the living personal God altogether.

This misconception has its main root in the crude metaphysics of spontaneous thought. This assumes that substance in general is changeless, and that change falls among the activities and properties. But a little reflection shows that an absolutely rigid substance cannot explain the changing activities of the thing. For every change in the activity or the manifestation, we must affirm a corresponding change in the thing itself. Changes among things must depend upon changes in things. What is true of all agents is true of God or the world-ground. God, as a rigid sameness of existence, would contain no explanation of the advancing cosmic movement, and would admit of no change in action and knowledge. In truth, as metaphysics shows, the changelessness of a being consists not in such an ontological rigidity or fixed monotony of being, but rather in the constancy and continuity of the law which rules its several states and changes. The unchangeability of God means only the constancy and continuity of the divine nature which exists through all the divine acts as their law and source. Metaphysics further shows that if we insist upon having some abiding and identical principle superior to change and constant in change, it can be found only in personality.   And here it does not consist in any rigid core of being, but rather in the extraordinary power of self-consciousness, whereby the being distinguishes itself from its states, and constitutes itself identical and abiding.   Where this is lacking, there may be a continuity of process, but nothing more.   The unchangeability is purely formal, as when a given note is constantly produced.

But in truth a variety of things are gathered up in this attribute.   Religious thought, as distinct from theological thought, has generally meant something distinct from the metaphysical formula.   One aim has been to affirm the independence and eternity of God in opposition to the dependence and brevity of man.   Again, the predicate has often been made to mean the ethical constancy of the divine activity, and to exclude all arbitrariness and caprice from the divine purposes.   In this last sense the attribute passes from the metaphysical into the ethical realm, and eludes any metaphysical deduction or justification.

§ 49. A third attribute is that of omnipresence. By crude thought this is often understood as implying extension of the subject. Space is supposed to exist as infinite room, which is then filled out with a boundless bulk; and this is omnipresence. This view is speculatively untenable, and is incompatible with the unity of the world-ground. Nothing that exists extended in space can be a unit; for in every such being it will always be possible to distinguish different parts which are either actually separate or are held apart and together only by the forces in them. In the latter case the body disappears into an aggregate of different forces, and in both cases its unity disappears. No more can such a thing be omnipresent in space. It can only be present in space part for part, or volume for volume, and hence there is no proper omnipresence. Omnipresence is real only as the entire being is present at any and every point; as the entire mind is present in each and all its thoughts.

Speculatively, then, the doctrine of omnipresence must take another form, and one mainly negative. We are able to act directly upon only a few things. These are said to be present to us. In other cases we can act only through media. These are said to be absent. If the interaction were equally direct and immediate in all cases there would be no ground for the distinction of present and absent. Thus space appears to us as a limitation, although space is really but the form under which our dynamic limitations appear. Omnipresence means a denial of these limitations. Immediate action means presence; immediate action which extends to all things means omnipresence. God, or the world-ground, therefore, as immanent in all things, is omnipresent. If, then, he wills to act upon anything, he has not to cross any distance, long or short, to reach it, and he is not compelled to use media; but his activity is rather immediately and completely present. Conversely, if the finite wishes to act upon God, say by prayer, neither the prayer nor the person need go wandering about to reach and find God; for we live and have our being in him; and he is an ever-present power in us. Only in this sense, which denies that space is a limitation or barrier for God, is the doctrine of omnipresence tenable. This view is made all the more necessary from the claim of metaphysics that space is no ontological reality, and has only a mental existence.

§ 50. The attribute of eternity has a variety of meanings. The first and lowest is that of unbegun and endless duration of existence. If time be an ontological fact, the world-ground must be eternal in this sense, for void time could never have produced anything. There is, too, a certain æsthetic value in the thought of endless duration which is not unworthy of the infinite. But in general, religious thinkers have been unwilling to identify the divine eternity with endless duration, but have rather sought to place it in opposition to all time as denoting an existence above and beyond all temporal limits and conditions. This is an attempt to conceive the divine relation to time like the divine relation to space, as a superior and transcendental one.

The common thought of the matter is that time exists as a boundless form, which God fills out with his duration, just as in the common thought he fills out space with his extension; but this is metaphysically as untenable in one case as in the other. Metaphysics shows that time itself is but the form of change, and not an independent reality upon which change depends and in which change occurs. Still this does not decide whether the world-ground is above the law of time; for the temporal form might still be a necessity of its existence.

The shortest way out is to call the world-ground the unconditioned, and then to deduce from this attribute its superiority to all conditions, temporal or otherwise. But this notion of the unconditioned is a somewhat vague one, and cannot be used without scrutiny. Thought can positively affirm an unconditioned being only in the sense of a being which does not depend on other beings; but such a being might still have profound internal limitations. The world-ground is, indeed, unconditioned by anything beyond itself; but it must be conditioned by its own nature in any case, and the question arises whether this conditioning involves temporal sequence in the infinite life itself. To say that it does would involve us in the gravest speculative difficulties. We should have to hold that the world-ground is subject to a law of development, and comes only gradually to itself, or, rather, that there is some constitutional necessity in the world-ground which forbids it always to be in full possession of itself. In fact we should have to limit to the extent of this necessity that free and self-centred cause which reason demands as the only adequate world-ground. In consequence reason will always assume that the world-ground is strictly unconditioned until some necessity is found for viewing it as conditioned. In this the mind is led on by its conception of the perfect, or by its need of ideal completeness. The result is not something which the mind can prove to be true, but which, in default of disproof, it is sure to assume.

With this assumption we may view the relation of the world-ground to time as follows: First, there are certain features in our relation to time which cannot be affirmed of the world-ground. Thus we are subject to slow development; we come gradually to self-possession; we grow old and pass away. This we express by saying that we are subject to temporal limits and conditions. In none of these respects can the unconditioned world-ground be subject to time, but must rather be non-temporal. A being which is in full possession of itself so that it does not come to itself successively, but forever is what it wills to be, is not in time so far as itself is concerned. Such a being would have a changeless knowledge and a changeless life. It would be without memory and expectation, yet in the absolute enjoyment of itself. For such a being the present alone would exist; its now would be eternal, and its name, I Am. For us the unconditioned world-ground, or God, is such a being; and he is not to be viewed as conditioned by time with regard to his own self-consciousness and self-possession. But only in the self-centred and self-equivalent personality can we transcend the conditions and the sphere of time. God in himself, then, is not only the eternal or ever-enduring; he is also the non-temporal, or that which transcends temporal limits and conditions.

But God is not merely the absolute person without a past and a future; he is also the founder and conductor of the world-process. This fact brings God into a new relation to time. This process is a developing, changing one, and hence is essentially in time. Hence the divine activity therein is essentially temporal. But here too there is a certain timeless element. As knowing all the phases and possibilities of the process, the divine knowledge of the system may be viewed as without succession, and hence as non-temporal. But as the chief agent in the process, and as ever adjusting his activity to the advancing process, both his activity and knowledge must be changing, and hence temporal. A changeless knowledge of an ideal is possible; but a changeless knowledge of a changing thing is a contradiction. A knowledge of reality must embrace it as it is; and if reality changes the knowledge must change to correspond. Unchangeability and non-temporality apply to God only in his relation to himself. They apply to his knowledge only as related to himself or to the ideal and the possible.

Finally, metaphysics makes the suggestion which may have some value; that the present in time, like the here in space, may be purely relative, and that there may be an all-embracing present as there is an all-embracing here. We find it utterly impossible to define the present except in relation to the real in experience. This reality does not occur in the present, but constitutes the present; and hence the suggestion becomes possible that there may be a grasp of reality which shall constitute it all present.

If this were allowed, the non-temporality of the world-ground would offer no difficulty.

§ 51. This brings us to the attribute of omniscience. It is a possible conception that intelligence plays only a co-ordinate, if not secondary, part in the world-ground. Our own knowledge reaches to only a small part of what takes place within us, and the rest is shrouded in mystery. It is conceivable that, in like manner, there should be in the world-ground a double realm, one of which is hidden from the scrutiny and control of intelligence. But this supposition is so destitute of positive grounds as to be quite gratuitous. If extended to cosmic action it would deprive us of the control of free intellect, which we have found necessary for understanding the cosmic order. Finally, it is at such war with the perfect ideal of the reason that it never has found acceptance with those who admit any intelligence in the world-ground at all. Still it is well to recognize that this demand for perfect knowledge rests rather upon a subjective ideal than upon objective grounds. We proceed to inquire how far such knowledge is self-consistent.

In interpreting omniscience, etymologizing has too often taken the place of philosophizing, and speculators have sought to determine the content of the idea by analyzing the word. But this process is delusive. No idea can be understood by studying the composition of the word, but only by reflecting upon the way in which the idea is reached. In the largest sense of the word, omniscience means a knowledge of all things and of all events, past, present, and future, necessary, and free alike. But we cannot affirm that this is possible on the sole strength of etymology. We must rather inquire whether this stretching of omniscience is not as untenable as the similar stretching of omnipotence when it is made to affirm the possibility of the contradictory. All allow that the contradictory is impossible; and hence we are not at liberty to include contradiction in our conception of the divine attributes. As omnipotence must be limited to the doable, so omniscience must be limited to the knowable. If, then, there be anything essentially unknowable, it must be beyond even omniscience.

A preliminary scruple exists concerning the divine knowledge of those forms of finite experience which cannot be ascribed to the Infinite. The totality of physical experiences seems to belong only to the finite; how, then, can the Infinite comprehend them? The work of the understanding in these cases consists entirely in classifying and naming; the thing itself is realized only in immediate experience. But if we are not willing to ascribe these experiences, as of physical pains, to God, and are also unwilling to deny him knowledge of the same, we must allow that there are modes of the divine knowing which we cannot comprehend. The contents of a sense which we do not possess are utterly unknowable to us, and yet by hypothesis the Infinite comprehends the finite experience without participation therein. The mystery involved in this assumption has led to many surmises in both theology and philosophy.

But the chief difficulty in omniscience concerns the foreknowledge of free choices. The past and present may be conceived to lie open to omniscience. The possible also may be fully known. The free creature can do nothing which was not foreseen as possible. Here, then, is a realm forever free from all enlargement and surprise. Here the parting of the ways begins.

A free act by its nature is a new beginning, and hence is not represented by anything before its occurrence which must lead to it. Hence a free act, until performed, is only a possibility, and not a fact. But knowledge must grasp the fact as it is, and hence it is held the act can be fore-known only as possible, and never as actual. Being only a possibility antecedently to its oc-currence, it must be known as such. On the other side it is held that, though only a possi-bility in itself, it may yet be known as one which will surely be realized. The knowledge in this case does not compel the fact, but fore-sees it, and leaves the fact as free as if unfore-seen.

Upon the possibility of such foreknowledge opinions still differ. Some have asserted fore-knowledge and denied freedom; others have as-serted freedom and denied foreknowledge; and still others have affirmed both. Both of the former classes agree in viewing freedom and foreknowledge as incompatible, and differ only as to which member of the antithesis they reject.

The difficulty in the last view is this: By definition a free act is an absolute beginning,

and as such is not represented by anything before its occurrence. We trace it to a specific
volition, and beyond that it has neither existence nor representation. But knowledge of a
future event always supposes present grounds
of knowing; and in the case of a free act there
are no such grounds. Hence a foreknowledge
of a free act is a knowledge without assignable
grounds of knowing. On the assumption of a
real time it is hard to find a way out of this
difficulty. Indeed, there would be no way out
unless we assume that God has modes of knowing which are inscrutable to us. A foreknowledge of freedom cannot be proved to be a contradiction; and on the other hand it cannot be
construed in its possibility. The doctrine of
the ideality of time helps us by suggesting the
possibility of an all - embracing present, or an
eternal now, for God. In that case the problem
vanishes with time its condition.

§ 52. The last attribute we consider is that of
omnipotence. This predicate implies what we
have before assumed from metaphysics, that the
world-ground is not a substance, but an agent;
not a stuff, but a cause; and the general aim

has been to affirm the absoluteness or uncondi-
tionedness of the world-ground.

Two tendencies appear in the common view
of the matter. One is to view God as able to
do the doable, but as limited by some necessities
which cannot be transcended. This view has
not satisfied either religious feeling or speculative thought; and the result has been to suggest the opposite view, according to which God
is lifted above all limits, and is able to do the
impossible as well as the possible. But if the
former view seemed tame, the latter seems to
be utter nonsense, and the death of reason itself.

We have already pointed out that necessity
has no positive meaning except as rational necessity. The question then concerns the relation of God to these necessities of reason, or, as
they are often called, the eternal truths. Is he
conditioned by them, or superior to them? We
shall need to move warily and with great circumspection to escape falling a prey to the
swarms of abstractions in which this realm
abounds.

§ 53. In speaking of the unity of the world-
ground we pointed out that it is incompatible

with any plurality of fundamental being. Hence it follows that truth and necessity themselves must in some way be founded in the world-ground. If we should assume a realm of truth to exist apart from being, it could have no effect in being unless we should further assume an interaction between it and being. But this would make truth a thing, and would compel the assumption of another being deeper than both truth and reality to mediate their interaction. At this point we fall an easy prey to our own abstractions. A law of nature is never the antecedent, but the consequence of reality. The real is first and only, and being what it is, its laws result as a consequence, or, rather, are but expressions of what the things are. Yet so easily do we mistake abstractions for things that, after we have gathered the laws from the things, we at once proceed to regard the things as the subjects, if not the products, of the laws they found. Then we speak of the reign of law; and thus by a double abstraction law is made to appear as a real sovereign apart from and above things, and as the expression of some fathomless necessity. Of course, when reality appears it has nothing to do but to fall into the

11

forms which the sovereign laws prescribe. Thus the cause is made subject to its own effects, and reality is explained as the result of its own consequences. The inverted nature of the thought is manifest. Natural laws are the consequences of reality, and never its grounds or anything apart from it.

The same is true for truth. Rational truth, as distinct from truth of contingent fact, is never anything more than an expression of the necessary relations of ideas, or of the way in which reason universally proceeds. As such it is nothing apart from the mind or antecedent to it, but is simply an expression of the mental nature. But we overlook this and abstract a set of principles which we call eternal truths, and erect into a series of fathomless necessities to which being can do nothing but submit. But the fictitious nature of this procedure is apparent. There is no realm of truth apart from the world-ground; and we must look in this being for the foundation of truth itself, and of all those principles whereby the distinctions of true and false, consistent and contradictory, possible and impossible, themselves exist. In a system in which these distinctions are already founded, they would be valid for all new events, not, however, as abstract necessities, but as actual laws of a real system.

It is partly oversight of this distinction which leads us to think that these principles precede reality. They do, indeed, precede specific events and condition them, and hence we fancy that they precede reality in general. A further fancy completes the illusion. When one speaks of truth as valid even in the void, he fails to see that his conception of the void is only a conception, and that he himself is present with all his ideas and laws of thought. And when along with his conception of the void he has other conceptions, and finds that the customary relations between them continue to exist, he fancies that he has truly conceived the void and has found that the laws of thought would be valid if all reality should vanish. But the illusion is patent. The whole art of finding what would be true in the void consists in asking what is now true for the thinking mind. The true void would be the undistinguishable nothing; and the ideal distinctions of truth and error would have no meaning, to say nothing of application. Hence we conclude that truth is not independent of the world-ground, but is in some way founded therein and dependent thereon.

§ 54. This dependence may be conceived in two ways. Truth may be viewed as founded in the nature of the world-ground, or as a creature of volition. The latter view has often appeared in theology, but is inconsistent with itself. The statement that God is arbitrary with regard to truth, that he can make or unmake it, assumes that truth exists and has a meaning apart from the divine volition. For why should the product of the creative act be called truth rather than error, unless it agree with certain fixed standards of truth with which error disagrees? Hence all such statements as that God can make the true false, or the possible impossible, imply that the standard of both exists independently of volition; and God is merely allowed to transfer objects back and forth across limits which are fixed in themselves.

The inconsistency of the negative form of statement is equally manifest. In order that truth shall be unmade or broken, it must first exist as truth. If any proposition which is to be broken were not in itself true, there would be no truth to break.   A proposition which is false cannot be made false, for it is false already. Hence, to make truth the creature of volition either denies truth altogether, or else it breaks down through its own self-contradiction.   But the aim of those who have held this view has never been to deny truth, but rather to exalt the absolute and unconditioned independence of God.

So, then, we object to the statement either that God makes truth or that he recognizes it as something independent of himself.   He is rather its source and foundation; and it, in turn, is the fixed mode of his procedure.   We may view rational principles as consequences or expressions of the divine nature, or as fundamental laws of the divine activity.   Both phrases have the same meaning.

§ 55. Many have objected to ascribing a nature of any kind to God as the source of the divine manifestation.   They have found in such a notion a limitation, and have held that God, as absolute, must give himself his own nature. There must be nothing constitutional with God, but all that he is must be a product of his absolute will. In himself God has been styled "the abyss," "the silence," "the super-essential," and many other verbal vacuities. This is due partly to a misunderstanding of the term, nature, and partly to an overstrained conception of absoluteness. We notice first the misunderstanding.

We finite beings are subject to development, and view our nature as the mysterious source of the movement. Again we inherit much, and we often sum up our inherited peculiarities as our nature. This nature too frequently appears as a limitation from which we would gladly escape. Thus a split arises in the soul. The free spirit has to struggle against a power which seems to be not of itself—an old man of the sea, or a body of death. In this sense a nature cannot be ascribed to an absolute being. Such a nature is essentially a limitation, and can belong only to the conditioned and finite.

But a nature in the sense of a fixed law of activity or mode. of manifestation involves no such limitation. This is best seen in a concrete case. Thinking, we say, is governed by the laws of thought. But these laws are not anything either out of the mind or in the mind. We feel them neither as an external yoke nor as an internal limitation. The reason is that they are essentially only modes of thought-activity, and are reached as formal laws by abstraction from the process of thinking. The basal fact is a thought-activity, and reflection shows that this has certain forms. These are next erected into laws and imposed on the mind; and then the fancy arises that they are limitations and hinderances to knowledge. In fact, however, they do not rule intellect, but only express what intellect is. Nor is the mind ever so conscious of itself as self-guiding and self-controlled as when conducting a clear process of thought. It would be a strange proposition to free the mind and enlarge knowledge by annulling the laws of thought.

This brings us to the overstraining mentioned. To deny a nature to God in the sense just described would be to cancel his existence altogether. For whatever is must be something, must be an agent, and must have a definite law of action. Without this the thought vanishes, and only a mental vacuum remains. This may indeed be filled up with words, but it acquires no substance thereby. To regard this definite law as a limitation is to make being itself a limitation. In that case we find true absoluteness only in pure indefiniteness and emptiness, and then there is no way back to definite existence again. Once in such a void, thought would remain there. This overstraining of absoluteness defeats itself. It cancels the absolute as a reality, and leads to the attempt to construct both the universe and the living God out of nothing. But when we say that the nature of a thing is a law, we must not think of the law as a thing in the thing, or even as ruling the thing. The thing itself is all; and the law is only an expression of what the thing is or of the way in which it proceeds.

We come here to a fact to which we have referred before, namely, the impossibility of dispensing with either necessity or freedom in a thought-system. To give freedom any significance it must be based on uniformity or fixity; and to give this fixity any value it must be allied with freedom. Unmixed necessity cancels reason. Pure arbitrariness cancels reason. It is only in the union of the two that the rational life is possible.

§ 56. Has, then, the divine will nothing to do with the divine existence? Does God find himself given to himself as an object, or is he, rather, his own cause? The answer must be both yes and no. The question really assumes that God as knowing and willing, is subsequent to himself as existing. Of course there is no temporal sequence, but only a logical one. God does not exist and then act, but exists only in and through his act. And this act, though not arbitrary, is also not necessary; or though necessary, it is also free. What this apparent contradiction means is this: Freedom and necessity are contradictory only as formal ideas, and are not mutually exclusive as determinations of being. Indeed, both ideas are at bottom abstractions from opposite sides of personal existence. We find an element of uniformity and fixity in our life, and this gives us the only positive idea of necessity which we possess. We find also a certain element of self-determination, and this is our idea of freedom. Reality, then, shows these formally opposite ideas united in actual existence, and reflection shows that both are necessary to rational existence. We have an illustration both of the meaning and of the possibility in our own life. The laws of thought are inviolable in the nature of reason. Volition can do nothing with them in the way of overthrow. And yet, though absolute and secure from all reversal, they do not of themselves secure obedience. The human soul does not become a rational soul by virtue of the law of reason alone; there is needed, in addition, an act of corresponding self-determination by the free spirit. Hence, while there is a necessity in the soul, it becomes controlling only through freedom; and we may say that every one must constitute himself a rational soul. How this can be is inconstruable, but none the less it is a fact. We come to our full existence only through our own act. What is true for ourselves in a limited degree, we may regard as absolutely true for God. At every point the absolute will must be present to give meaning to the otherwise powerless necessities of the Divine Being. In this sense we may say, with Spinoza, that God is the cause of himself. He incessantly constitutes himself the rational and absolute spirit. God is absolute will or absolute agent, forever determining himself according to rational and eternal principles.

CHAPTER V.

GOD AND THE WORLD.

Thus far we have considered mainly the attributes of God in himself; we have now to consider his cosmical relations. Of course it is not our aim to tell how God produces the world, or how the world depends on him, but only to find what general thought we must form of their mutual relations. By the world, here, we mean all finite existence. Two general classes of views exist: theistic and pantheistic. Pantheism makes the world either a part of God or a necessary consequence of the divine nature. Theism holds that the world is a free act and creation by God. We consider pantheism first.

§ 57. The view that the world is a part of God is the common factor in all theories of emanation, ancient and modern. As the waves are a part of the ocean, or, better still, as each finite space or time is a part of the one infinite space or time, so each finite thing is a part or phase of the one infinite existence. In each of these views God is regarded as world-substance rather than first cause; and this substance is conceived as a kind of plastic stuff or raw material which, like clay, can be variously fashioned, and which is at least partly exhausted in its products. Sometimes the view is less coarse, and God is conceived as the background of the world, something as space is the infinite background and possibility of the figures in it. Sometimes God is said to produce or emit the world from himself, or by a process of self-diremption to pass from his own unity into the plurality of cosmic existence. The finite, on the other hand, is a part, or mode, or emanation of the infinite, and shares in the infinite substance. Whether the world is eternal is not decided. Some will have it to be an eternal part and factor of God, while others think it as made out of God.

All views of this class are products of the imagination and result from the attempt to picture that which is essentially unpicturable. When we try to conceive the origin of the world we are tempted to form the fancy of some back-lying plastic substance of which the world is made, and then the imagination is satisfied. Either we refer the world to some pre-existent stuff, or we regard it as pre-existing itself in some potential form. Then its production becomes either the working over of a given stuff or a letting loose of potentialities.

Views of this class are as obnoxious to reason as they are dear to the irrational fancy. Metaphysics shows that reality is never a stuff, but an agent. Nor does an agent have any substance in itself whereby it exists, but by virtue of its activity it is able to assert itself as a determining factor in existence, and thus only does it acquire any claim to be considered real. To explain the universe we need not a substance, but an agent; not substantiality, but causality. The latter expresses all the meaning of the former, and is free from misleading sense-implications. Metaphysics further shows that every agent is a unit, uncompounded and indivisible. God, then, is not the infinite stuff or substance, but the infinite cause or agent, one and indivisible. From this point all the previous views of the relation of God to the world disappear of themselves. He has no parts and is not a sum. Hence the world is no part of God, nor an emanation from him, nor a sharer in the divine substance; for all these views imply the divisibility of God and also his stuff-like nature. His necessary unity forbids all attempts to identify him with the world, either totally or partially. If the finite be anything real, it must be viewed, not as produced from God, but as produced by God; that is, as created. Only creation can reconcile the reality of the finite with the unity of the infinite. For the finite, if real, is an agent, and as such it cannot be made out of anything, but is posited by the infinite.

Similar objections lie against all views which speak of the world as a mode of God. This phrase, in its common use, is allied to the imagination, and is based upon the notion of a passive substance. The thought commonly joined with it is that each thing is a particular and separate part of the infinite, as each wave is not a phase of the entire sea, but only of the part comprised in the wave itself. But metaphysics further shows that the unity of being is compatible with plurality of attributes only as each is an attribute of the whole thing. Any conception of diverse states which are states of only a part of the thing would destroy its unity. The entire being must be present in each state; and this cannot be so long as the notion of quantity is applied to the problem. The only way in which a being can be conceived as entire in every mode, is by dropping all quantitative and spatial conceptions and viewing the being as an agent, and the modes as forms of its activity. If, then, finite things are modes of the infinite, this can only mean that they are acts of the infinite, or modes of agency.

Another conception of this relation has been ventured, based on the relation of the universal to the particulars subsumed under it, and more especially on the relation of the universal reason to the individual mind. As reason is the same in all, and as no one can claim a monopoly of it, but only a participation in it, we may say that the universal reason is the reality, and that the finite mind exists only in and through it as one of its phases or manifestations. But this is only an echo of the scholastic realism. Class terms denote no possible existence, and have reality only in the specific existences from which they are abstracted.

§ 58. Two conceptions of the finite are logically possible. First, we may regard it as only a
mode of the divine activity and without any
proper thinghood. Secondly, we may view it as
a proper thing, not only as an act of God, but as
a substantial product. The former conception
is illustrated by the relation of thoughts to the
mind. These are not modes of mind, but mental
acts. They are not made out of anything, but
the thinking mind gives them existence. At the
same time, they are not things in the mind, but
exist only in and through the act which creates
them.

The decision between these views can be
reached only as we find, in the finite, things
which can know themselves as things. At first
sight, indeed, things and substances appear to
be given in immediate perception ; but psychology shows that the objects of perception are primarily never more than our own conceptions
and representations which have been objectified
under the forms of space and time, substance
and attribute, cause and effect, etc. They represent only the way in which the mind reacts
against a series of incitements from without.
Metaphysics further shows that the external

fact is totally unlike the appearance; and when
these considerations are followed out we reach
the insight that true substantial existence, in distinction from phenomenal existence, can be pred-
icated only of persons.   Only selfhood serves to
mark off the finite from the infinite, and only
the finite spirit attains to substantial otherness
to the infinite.   The impersonal finite has only
such otherness as a thought or act has to its
subject.

This view does not commend itself to spontaneous thought, and is questioned by many in the
name of common-sense.   The objections commonly rest upon misapprehension.   Our sense-
experience puts us in connection with a system
of things.   Concerning this system, we may ask
whether it depends on us, as the illusions of the
madman depend on his distempered mind, or
whether it is independent of us and our perception.   The common conception of idealism is
that it affirms the former view.   This is one of
the chronic misconceptions for which, when once
established, there seems to be no exorcism.   No
rational idealist, however, has ever held such a
view.   He believes, as much as any one, that the
system of experience is no product of our own,

12

and that it exists for all. He only raises the question what this system may be in its essential nature. The realist proposes the conception of a brute existence as expressing its ultimate nature; but the idealist has no difficulty in showing that such a conception is only the realist's theory, and not a fact of immediate experience, and that this theory, moreover, is quite unable to do the work assigned it. And the realist himself is compelled to relax his theory when he comes to consider the relation of God and the world. Of course the imagination has no difficulty in construing this relation as a spatial one—as one of mutual inclusion and exclusion — but not much reflection is needed to show the impossibility of such a view or the contradictions involved in it. The most striking advantages of the realistic view for the imagination become its chief embarrassments for reflective thought. But this question is aside from our theistic argument. This remains the same whatever our attitude towards the realistic controversy.

§ 59. In any case the spirit must be viewed as created. It is not made, for making implies a pre-existent stuff. Creation means to posit something in existence which before was not. Concerning it two consistent questions are possible. (1.) Who is the agent? (2.) How is it possible? To the first question the answer is, God. To the second there is no rational answer

Besides these consistent questions, various inconsistent ones are asked, as, for instance: What is the world made " out of"? The common answer is, out of nothing. Both question and answer are worthy of each other. Both are haunted by the notion of a pre-existent stuff, and, to complete the absurdity, the answer suggests nothing as that stuff; as if by some process God fashioned the nothing into something. The old saw, from nothing nothing comes, is also played off against creation, but without effect. The truth therein is merely that nothing can ever produce, or be formed into anything. But theism does not teach that nothing produces something, but rather that God, the all-powerful, has caused the world to exist. No more does theism hold that God took a mass of nothing and made something out of it, but rather that he caused a new existence to begin, and that, too, in such a way that he was no less after creation than before. God neither made the world from nothing as a raw material, nor from himself; both notions are absurd; but he caused that to be which before was not. Of course, we have no recipe for this process. Creation is a mystery; but any other view is a contradiction of thought itself. Creation is the only conception which reconciles the unity of God with the existence of the finite. Perhaps, too, we need not be especially troubled at the mystery, as mystery is omnipresent; and besides, creation is not our affair.

Some speculators have sought relief from the mystery of creation in the claim that the world was not made from nothing, but from the potentialities of the divine nature. The only intelligible meaning of this view is that the world existed as a conception in the divine thought before it became real. This conceptual existence constituted its potentiality, but this in no way shows how that which existed as conception was posited in reality. For the rest, the claim in question is only a form of words of learned sound but without meaning.

§ 60. The world depends upon a divine activity, and is not a mode of the infinite substance. But this also admits of a double in-

terpretation. We may regard this activity as
a necessary consequence of the divine nature,
or as resting upon the divine will. The former
view is held by all the higher forms of pantheism, and even some theists have held that God
must create. This view also is double, according to our thought of being in general. In one
view God exists as the all-conditioning substance, and the world, as its necessary implication, co-exists eternally with it. Spinoza's doctrine is the best expression of this view. But
this conception compels us either to affirm that
all things are eternal, or else to declare change
to be an unaccountable illusion of the finite.
This view, which might be called static pantheism, has generally been exchanged for another,
which might be called dynamic pantheism. In
the latter view the infinite is forever energizing
according to certain laws, and producing thereby
a great variety of products. But these laws are
throughout expressions of its nature and admit
of no change. The world-order is the divine
nature, and, conversely, the divine nature is the
world-order. Hence pantheists of this order
have always been the stoutest opponents of
miracles, for miracles imply a will apart from

and above nature.　If the world-order were really the divine nature, then, of course, God could not depart from that order without denying himself. This conviction is further strengthened by the natural tendency of the untaught mind to mistake the uniformities of experience for necessities of being; and thus the world-order is finally established as necessarily invariable, the mind not recognizing its own shadow.　This is the view which underlies all schemes of philosophic evolution, and a large part of current scientific speculation, or rather speculation on the supposed basis of scientific facts and principles. While static pantheism says, In the beginning was the eternal substance or the eternal reason co-existing changelessly with all its implications; dynamic pantheism says, In the beginning was force, necessary and persistent, and by its inherent necessity forever generating law and system.　When this view is combined with the impersonality and unconsciousness of the world-ground, it becomes identical with vulgar atheism.　The world-ground is simply the unitary principle and basal reality of the cosmos, and is exhausted in its cosmic manifestation. There is immanence without transcendence;

and God and the world are but opposite names for the same thing.

§ 61. Static pantheism is an untenable abstraction which, if allowed, would bring the universe to a standstill and load thought with illusion. It would give us a rigid and resting being from which all time and change would be excluded, and which could in no way be connected with our changing experience. If we should call that experience delusion, the delusion itself would be as unaccountable as the fact. On this rock the Eleatic philosophy was wrecked, and here, too, Spinoza's system went to pieces. The truth, then, in pantheism, if there be any, lies in dynamic pantheism. But even this view has but scanty value, and this value lies in its emphasis of law in opposition to a blind and reckless arbitrariness. For the rest, pantheism is unsatisfactory in all respects. First, it is ethically objectionable, because it leads to a complete determinism, both in God and man. All things happen by necessity, and nothing is the outcome of proper prevision and purpose. The world and all its details are determined from everlasting. There is no room for freedom, hence none for purpose, and hence none for any rational distinction of good and evil.

The view is also speculatively obnoxious in the following respects:

1. It is unclear. It provides only for the world-order and does not recognize its details. But the world-order, as a system of general laws, accounts for no specific fact whatever. We must reckon, then, not only the world-order to the divine nature, but also the cosmic details. And since these are incessantly shifting, the divine nature, which is their ground, must also be shifting, and hence a temporal thing. Thereby the infinite is degraded to a temporal existence and its absoluteness disappears; for only the self-determining can be absolute.

2. Self-determination being denied, we must find some ground for the changing activity of the infinite; and this must be found in some mechanism in the infinite whereby its states interact and determine the outcome. This view carried out would cancel the unity of the infinite altogether. We might continue to speak of unity, but we should be quite unable to tell in what that unity consisted. As we have al-

ready pointed out, the free and conscious self is the only real unity of which we have any knowledge, and reflection shows that it is the only thing which can be a true unity.

3. We have seen that the alleged necessity of natural laws and products is purely hypothetical. No reflection upon necessary truth shows the present order to be a necessary implication in any respect.

4. We have further seen that every system of necessity overturns reason itself.

On all these grounds we hold that God is free in his relation to the world, and that the world, though conditioned by the divine nature, is no necessary product thereof, but rather rests upon the divine will. To carry the world into God is to carry time and evolution into God; and the notion of an evolving, developing God does not commend itself to speculative thought. Again, to carry the actual world into God with all its antitheses of good and evil, and its boundless wastes of insignificance and imperfection, would be to degrade the theistic idea to about the level of the Platonic demiurge. Everything would be divine but God.

In concluding that God is free in his relation

to the world, we abandon all hope of a speculative deduction of creation. Such hope has often
been entertained, and numberless attempts have
been made to realize it. Inasmuch as we conclude from the world to God, we must be able
to conclude from God to the world. Sometimes
the matter has been made very easy by defining
creation as essential to the divine nature; and
then the conclusion has been drawn that God
without the world would be a contradiction. In
addition to being failures, these attempts spring
from a speculative lust for understanding and
construing, which fails to grasp the conditions
of understanding. In this respect they are on
a par with the infantile wisdom which asks,
Who made God?

§ 62. The world, then, depends on the divine
will. In estimating this result, care must be
taken not to apply to the divine willing the
limitations of the human. As in human consciousness there are many features which are
not essential to consciousness, and which arise
from our limitations, so in human willing there
are many features which are not essential to
willing, and which result from our finiteness.

Since we get our objects of volition gradually and by experience, we tend to think of will as a momentary activity which comes into our life now and then, but which, for the most part, is quiescent. In this way we come to think of an act of will as having nothing to do with the maintenance of a fixed state, but only as producing a change; or if it should look to the preservation of a given state, it would only be as that state might be threatened by something external. And so, finally, it comes to pass that we think of willing as something necessarily temporal or beginning. When, then, we speak of the world as depending on the divine will, the imagination finds it difficult to grasp this thought without assuming an empty time before its origination.

But these features of human willing are not to be transferred to God without inspection. To begin with, willing does not necessarily imply beginning. In studying the divine omnipotence we saw that God's will in reference to himself must be eternal; that is, it is as unbegun as God, being but that free self-determination whereby God is God. It is only in relation to the world that God's will can be temporal; and here, too, there is an essential difference. We come only gradually to a knowledge of our aims; but this cannot be affirmed of God. We have seen that in his absolute self-knowledge and self-possession God has neither past nor future. Hence the ideals of the divine will are also eternal in the divine thought. The will to create, however, is differently regarded. Some view it as an eternal predicate of God, and others view it as a temporal predicate.

Still another distinction between our will and the creative will must be noticed. With us to will is not necessarily to fulfil; and thus we come to think that in addition to the will there must also be a special activity of realization. Some have carried this conception over to God, and have affirmed the will to create to be eternal, while the execution is temporal. But this view confounds intention with will, and for the rest, is false. This feature of our willing is due altogether to our finiteness. Our willing, in fact, extends only to our mental states, and is not absolute even there. For the production of effects in the outer world we depend on something not ourselves; and as this is not always

subservient to us, we come to distinguish between volition and realization. Again, we find
that we cannot always control our thoughts,
because they are partly due to external causes;
and in the struggle which thus arises we find
additional ground for distinguishing the will
and the realization. Finally, our control of the
body is attended by many feelings of strain and
effort, and these we carry into the idea of will
itself, where it by no means belongs. These
feelings are effects of muscular tension resulting from our will, but they are no part of the
will itself. None of these elements can be
transferred to God. He is unconditioned by
anything beyond himself. He is the absolutely
self-determining, and with him willing must be
identical with realization.

§ 63. Two views, we said, are held of the will
to create, some making it an eternal and others
only a temporal predicate of God. Of these two
views the latter is the more easily realized by
the imagination. By its affirmation of an empty
time before the creative act, that act is made
to appear more like an act than an eternal
doing would be, and at the same time the view

marks off creation as an act of will more clearly from the opposite doctrine, which makes creation a necessary consequence of the divine nature. This, however, is only an aid to the imagination. If the Creator be free, he is eternally free. He did not first exist and then become free, but his freedom is coexistent with himself; and hence his free doing may coexist with himself. There is nothing in the notion of eternal creation which is incompatible with divine freedom or with the absolute dependence of the world on the divine will. The notion of a temporal creation has the disadvantage also of raising certain troublesome questions, such as, What was God doing in the eternity before creation? or, Why did creation take place when it did, and not at some other time? We cannot fill up this time with a divine self-evolution, as if God were gradually coming to himself and getting ready to create, for this would cancel his absoluteness and reduce him to a temporal being. Some of the more naïve speculators have thought to fill up the time before creation by a series of previous creations—a suggestion which shows more appreciation of the difficulty of the problem than of the re-

quired solution. It seems, then, that no reason
for delay can be found in God, and certainly
none can be found in time itself, since one moment of absolute time is like any other; and
hence, finally, it seems that a temporal creation
must be an act of pure arbitrariness. On all
these accounts many theologians have declared
for an eternal creation, and have further declared creation to mean not temporal origination, but simply and only the dependence of the
world on God.

But, on the other hand, the notion of an
eternal creation of the world is not without
its difficulties, partly real and partly imaginary.
To begin with the latter, it is said that the cosmic process is a changing one, and hence temporal and hence begun. The answer is that
change does not take place in time, but founds
time, so that time is only the form of change.
Hence temporality and change are identical.
But temporality in this sense is simply a mode
of existence, and its antithesis is not the unbegun but the changeless. Viewed as enduring,
the changing process may be as eternal as its
cause.

This conception of time gives a somewhat

different aspect to the question. Metaphysics
shows that time cannot be a proper ontological
reality, but is only the form of change in general. The cosmic process is not in time, but by
its incessant change it produces the form of
time. God, however, as the absolute person, is
non-temporal and exists in absolute self-possession without past or future. Hence time began with the cosmic process, and the questions,
What was God doing before creation? and Why
did he create when he did? have no meaning.
In his absolute self-related existence, God is
timeless. Hence he did not create at a certain
point of absolute time, but he created and thus
gave both the world and time their existence.
If, then, we view the world as begun, it is
strictly absurd to ask when or at what moment of the eternal flow of time did God create.
There is no such flow; and hence creation did
not take place at any moment. In the beginning God created, for creation was the beginning even of time itself.

§ 64. Many attempts have been made to prove
eternal creation to be a contradiction. These
generally rest on the assumption of a real time,

and fall into contradiction with themselves. The claim is that the world must have had a beginning in time, while the arguments employed prove with equal cogency that time itself must have had a beginning. This is the case even with Kant, whose famous antinomy is no more efficient against the eternity of the world than it is against the eternity of time. But no one who admits an infinite past time can find any good reason for denying that something may always have been happening in it. Every believer in necessity must hold that something has always been going on; and every theist must allow that something may always have been going on. There is no apriori reason in theism for denying that the cosmic process may be coeternal with God.

The difficulties commonly urged depend on the contradiction said to inhere in the notion of an infinite elapsed time. But this arises from overlooking the sense in which past time is said to be infinite. This infinity means simply that past time cannot be exhausted by any finite regress. Past time is infinite just as space in any direction is infinite. In the former case no regress will find a beginning,

13

just as in the latter case no progress will find an end. If, now, time were anything capable of real objective existence, its past infinity, in the sense described, would offer no difficulty to thought; indeed, it would rather seem to be a necessary affirmation. Such difficulty as might arise would be due to confounding thought and imagination. The imagination cannot represent either space or time as unlimited, but thought cannot conceive either as limited. But with infinite time and the eternal God as data, there seems to be no reason for denying the possibility of a cosmic process extending throughout the infinite time.

Some further objections are offered, based on the nature of number. Number is necessarily finite, and hence anything to which number applies must be finite also. But number applies to time as its measure, and hence time must be finite, and hence must have a beginning. Such argument, however, puzzles rather than convinces. To begin with, the necessary finiteness of number means only that any number whatever admits of increase. But it is entirely compatible with this finitude that the number should not admit of exhaustion in any finite time. If we suppose time to be real and infinite, then in the past time a definite number of units have passed away; but that number does not admit of expression in finite terms. It is constantly growing, to be sure, because time is constantly passing. In no other sense need it be finite. If it be said that the very nature of a series demands a beginning, as there can be no second without a first, we need to consider whether such application of number to the boundless continuum of time is not as relative to ourselves as its similar application to space. For our apprehension we have to set up axes of reference in both cases; but we are not able to say that the fact itself depends upon those devices by which we conceive it. The celestial horizon and equator do not make the motions and positions which they enable us to grasp and measure. The argument from number proves the finitude of space quite as cogently as that of time. But if we allow that time is infinite, and claim only that the cosmic process in time must be finite, we fall into a curious antinomy. On the one hand, it seems clear that the Eternal God may always have been doing something; but on the other hand, owing to the potency of number, God must have waited for the past eternity to elapse before he could do anything. The truth is, we have here the opposition between time as thought and time as imagined, to which reference has already been made. Oversight of this distinction vitiates not a few of the traditional arguments for a first cause. Our inability to represent an eternal process is taken for the proof of a beginning.

But it is time to return from this long excursion. Our view of time empties most of these questions of all significance. We need not concern ourselves with what God was doing in the long eternity before creation; for there was no such eternity. There was simply the self-existent, self-possessing, timeless God, whose name is I Am, and whose being is without temporal ebb and flow. Temporal terms have meaning only within the cosmic process itself, and are altogether empty when applied to the absolute God. And within the cosmic process itself temporal relations are but the form under which we represent the unpicturable dynamic relations among the things and phases of that process.

§ 65. The conception of creation as a free act and not as a necessary evolution of the nature of the world-ground, forbids all attempts to identify the world with God. But speculative thought has been prolific in attempts to understand the manner and motive of creation. A superficial type of speculation has sought to explain the manner by a great variety of cosmogonies, some of which are still in fashion. None of these have either religious or speculative significance. They relate only to the transforming and combining of given material, and say nothing concerning its origination. For understanding the origin of the creative act, we have only the analogy of our own experience, according to which we first form conceptions and then realize them. Hence the divine understanding has been distinguished from the divine will, and a kind of division of labor has been made between them. The understanding furnishes the conception of all possibilities, and from these the divine wisdom chooses the best for realization by the divine will. Many scruples have been raised concerning this distinction, on the ground that in God knowing and willing must be identical; but this identity is secured only by defining each term so as to include the other. In both cases, however, we have to leave out those features of our knowing and willing which arise from our limitations. In general the identification of knowing and willing in God confounds synchronism with identity. In knowing which looks towards doing there is no assignable reason why the doing should be postponed, and thus we are led to view them as contemporaneous. But knowing and willing as mental functions remain as distinct as ever. Besides, God's knowledge extends to the evil as well as the good; does he therefore will the evil?

Concerning the motive of creation pure speculation can say nothing positive. It can only point out that if the divine absoluteness is to be maintained, this motive must not lie in any lack or imperfection of the Creator. For positive suggestion we must have recourse to our moral and religious nature; and this refuses to be satisfied with any lower motive than ethical love. This fact, together with the positive teachings of Christianity, has led to many attempts to deduce the system as an outcome of love; but the success has been very slight. We

are so little able to tell apriori what that love
implies that we cannot even adjust a large part
of actual experience to the conception of any
kind of love, ethical or otherwise. It only remains that we believe in love as the source of
creation and the essence of the divine nature,
without being in any way able to fix its implications.

§ 66. The world was produced by the divine
will, but this does not determine its present relation to that will. Concerning this there are
two extreme views and an indefinite number of
intermediate ones. One extreme, deism, regards
the world as needing only to be created, being
able to exist thereafter entirely on its own
account. The other extreme finds so little
substantiality in the world as to regard its
continued existence as a perpetual creation.
Between these extremes lie the views which,
against deism, maintain an activity of conservation distinct from that of creation, and which,
on the other hand, refuse to identify creation
and conservation.

The deistic view sets up nature as an independent power with laws and rights of its own,

while God appears as an absentee and without any administrative occupation so far as nature is concerned. The impossibility of this conception has already appeared. No finite thing has any metaphysical rights of its own whereby it becomes an obstacle or barrier in any sense to God. Both laws and things exist or change solely because of the demands of the divine plan. If this calls for fixedness, they are fixed; if it calls for change, they change. They have in themselves no ground of existence so as to be a limit for God; because they are nothing but the divine purpose flowing forth into realization. If natural agents endure it is not because of an inherent right to existence, but because the creative will constantly upholds them. If in the cosmic movement the same forces constantly appear working according to the same laws, this is not because of some eternal persistence of force and law, but because it lies in the divine plan to work in fixed forms and methods for the production of compound effects. In a word, the continuity of natural processes upon which physical science is based is admitted as a fact, but not as a fact which accounts for itself or which rests upon some metaphysical necessity, but rather as a fact which depends at every moment upon the divine will, and which only expresses the consistency of the divine methods. As against deism, then, we hold that the world is no self-centred reality, independent of God, but is simply the form in which divine purpose realizes itself. It has no laws of its own which oppose a bar to the divine purpose, but all its laws and ongoings are but the expression of that purpose. In our dealing with nature we have to accommodate ourselves to its laws, but with God the purpose is original, the laws are its consequence. Hence the system of law is itself absolutely sensitive to the divine purpose, so that what that purpose demands finds immediate expression and realization, not in spite of the system, but in and through the system.

The view which identifies conservation with perpetual creation is manageable only when applied to the physical system. Here form and law are the only fixed elements we can find; and metaphysics makes it doubtful whether there can be others. In that case the physical order becomes simply a process which exists only in its perpetual ongoing. It has the identity of a musical note, and, like such a note, it exists only on condition of being incessantly and continuously reproduced. But we cannot apply this view to the world of spirits without losing ourselves in utterly unmanageable difficulties.

We seem, then, shut up to distinguish creation from preservation. But the nature of this distinction eludes all apprehension. We are led here to affirm something whose nature and method are utterly opaque to our thought. On the one hand, we have a measure of self-hood and self - control. This fact constitutes our claim to be considered realities. On the other hand, we are forced to admit that our existence forever depends on some absolute existence. How these two facts coexist is perhaps the deepest mystery of speculation. Possibly the ideality of time might serve to relieve the difficulty involved in distinguishing creation and preservation.

§ 67. If the physical system only were concerned, nothing more need be added about the relation of the world to God. He is its creator and conserver, and we should add nothing in calling him its ruler or governor. Even realism regards the world of things as receiving its law from God, and as unable in any way to depart from it. Such things need no government; or, rather, government has no meaning when applied to them. We can speak of government only where there are beings which by a certain independence threaten to withdraw themselves from the general plan which the ruler aims to realize. We find the proper subjects of a divine government only in finite spirits, as only these have that relative independence over against God which the idea of government demands.

The notion of a divine government, then, implies free spirits as its subjects. But freedom in itself is a means only and not an end. Apart from some good which can be realized only by freedom, a free world is no better than a necessary one. Hence the notion of a world-government acquires rational meaning only as some supreme good exists which is to be the outcome of creation, and which, therefore, gives the law for all personal activity. A world-government implies a world-goal which, in turn, implies a world-law. A cosmic movement without direction and aim could not be the outcome of a self-respecting intelligence.

What, then, is that great end which all free beings should serve? Nature shows us numberless particular ends, but none of these have supreme worth, and most of them have no assignable worth. So far as observation goes, the ends realized in nature are generally so insignificant that they seem to add nothing to the perfection of the world, and in many cases they even appear as blemishes. Observation discovers no supreme end. The cosmos as a whole does not seem to set very definitely in any direction, and presents a drifting movement rather than a fixed course. Nor can we find the aim of the cosmic movement in any development of the world-ground, as that would reduce it to a temporal existence. But if we insist on having a world-goal, we can find a sufficient one only in the moral realm. A community of moral persons, obeying moral law and enjoying moral blessedness, is the only end which could excuse creation or make it worth while. Hence the notion of a moral government leads at once to the ethical realm, and implies notions foreign to metaphysics. If one has not these notions there can be no question of such a government, and theistic philosophy closes with considering the causal relation of God to the world.

§ 68. If we suppose the world of things to contain the reason of its existence within itself, there is no reason why the fixed order of antecedence and sequence should ever be departed from. In such a world any one state would be as good as any other, and new departures would have no significance. But a world of things which is to minister to a world of persons must not be thus rigid. It must be capable of taking up new factors or of receiving impulses from without. Only on this condition can it become the servant of finite intelligence. The actual system is such a system. It is perpetually taking on new modifications which are not the results of the antecedent states of the system, but which have their source in human volition. This volition, however, breaks no laws, but realizes itself through the laws. As soon as the volitional impulse is given, the effect enters into the great web of law and is carried out by the same.

This fact suggests a means of conceiving the method of the divine government. In a world of free beings there may be at times a departure from the ideal order of things, and to remedy this it may be necessary to meet it by changes in things which are not consequents of the antecedent states of the system. As the system is constantly taking on modifications which have their source in human volition, so it may be constantly taking on modifications which have their source in special divine volition. In that case effects would be produced which the system in its accustomed movement would not realize. Such effects involve no general suspension of natural laws, nor even a break of phenomenal continuity. They would arise apparently as the result of familiar natural processes although really rooted in a special divine volition. This conception of miracle provides for a divine government as distinct from the simple maintenance of a rigid order. Miracles as signs we have no call to discuss.

This general conception of interpolated effects has been stoutly rejected. So far as this rejection rests on atheistic assumptions, it does not exist for theism. So far as it proceeds from theists, it generally depends on the deistic conception of the relation of God and the world. God being an absentee, and the world being able to take care of itself, any modification appears as an "interference;" and as interfering often denotes a morally reprehensible procedure, there seems to be no help for rejecting the notion. In truth, the "interference" does no more violence to the system than do the analogous interferences of human volition. It seems permissible, then, to hold that what is possible with man may be possible with God. God, then, may be present in human history, guiding the world, raising up leaders, giving direction to public thought, purifying the receptive and willing heart, answering prayer according to his wisdom, and scourging public and private wickedness; yet without in any way breaking through the fixed phenomenal order.

But this only suggests a possibility and a method of conceiving how the divine government may coexist with fixed laws. The reality of the fact is another matter. If there be any reason for affirming it, speculation has no word of valid objection. It is plain, however, that such interventions must be sought chiefly in

the life of the spirit. Our freedom produces
only slight modifications in the outer world and
none in its laws. These need no change; and
it is hard to see of what use such change would
be if it were real. The modifying activity of
God doubtless finds its chief field in the inner
life, and here not in the way of using the spirit
as a passive instrument, but rather by furnish-
ing it with special incitements to activity which
neither the outer world nor the mental mechanism provides. But even this directing activity
takes place without any apparent irruption from
without and without destroying the apparent
continuity of psychological law.

§ 69. The discussion of miracle has proceed-
ed thus far on the realistic conception of the
cosmos. From my own metaphysical standpoint the question assumes a somewhat different form. In this view the cosmos contains
two factors, elementary forms of action and
laws for their combination. These laws are
fixed; but the forms of action are simply what
the divine purpose at any moment demands.
They represent, therefore, nothing fixed once
for all, so that from their state at any one mo-

ment we could deduce their state at all other moments. They are not, then, rigid fixities, but flowing expressions of the divine plan; and to know them we must know the plan and purpose which they express. They are forever becoming that which the Creator wills them to be. Here is where power has its seat and the road by which purpose marches to its realization. But with this conception of the divine immanence and of the absolute dependence of the system in all respects upon the divine purpose, the question of miracle loses all special significance. Nature becomes, not a self-enclosed existence, but only a general term for the established order of procedure; and a natural event is one in which familiar processes can be traced, or which can be connected with other events according to general laws. The miraculous, on the other hand, would have no such connection; but both the natural and the miraculous alike would have their root in the supernatural. Finally, we may question even the existence of laws except as formal and subjective. There is not first a system of general laws into which effects are afterwards interjected; but there is the actual system of re-

14

ality, upheld and maintained by the immanent God. For our thought this system admits of being analyzed into universal laws on the one hand and particular effects on the other; but in fact this is only a logical separation. The effects are no more consequences of the laws than the laws are consequences of the effects. The analyses and devices of discursive thought do not give us reality in its actual existence, but only a formal equivalent for purposes of our calculation. It is plain that in this view neither religion nor speculation can have any special interest in scientific cosmogonies, evolutionary or otherwise. These relate only to the method of cosmic procedure, and throw no light on the nature of the agent at work.

CHAPTER VI.

THE WORLD-GROUND AS ETHICAL.

THE attributes thus far considered are purely metaphysical and concern only the understanding. They are such properties as the speculative intellect must affirm in dealing with the problem of the universe and its ground. But if we should stop here we should not attain to any properly religious conception, but only to the last term of metaphysical speculation. A good example of this is furnished by Aristotle, with whom the idea of God has a purely metaphysical function and significance. God appears as prime mover, as self-moved, as the primal reason, etc., but not as the object of love and trust and worship.

But the human mind in general has not been content with a metaphysical conception of God, but has rather demanded a religious one. And the latter conception has always been first and not second. The metaphysical thought instead of being the foundation upon which the religious thought was built, has rather been reached by later analysis as an implication of the religious conception. The race has been universally religious, but only moderately metaphysical.

From the religious standpoint the important attributes concern the divine character or ethical nature. We have now to inquire for the ground of their affirmation.

§ 71. If we accept the mental ideal of a perfect being as the ground of the universe the question is settled at once. Moral qualities are the highest. The true, the beautiful, and the good love goodness and righteousness; these are the only things that have absolute sacredness and unconditional worth. The thought of a perfect being in which these qualities should be lacking, or present in only an imperfect degree, would be an intellectual, æsthetic, and moral absurdity of the first magnitude. But this demand for faith in the ideal when thus boldly made is apt to stagger us, and we prefer to reach the result in somewhat obscure manner. When we are told that the problem of knowledge demands the assumption of a universe transparent to our reason, so that what the laws of our thought demand the universe cannot fail to fulfil, we are staggered and have many doubts and scruples. So large an assumption is not to be made without due wariness and circumspection. But we make the assumption piecemeal, without a single critical qualm. In the actual study of nature, in dealing with specific problems, we assume the principle in question as a matter of course. It is only when stated in its abstract universality that it appals us. It is so with the larger ideal of the perfect being. We assume it implicitly and upon occasion, but we do not like to have it brought out in sharp abstract statement. Here, then, is a psychological limitation of the average mind which must be regarded. We shall find it interesting, however, to note the way in which the ideal determines our reasoning.

§ 72. There is no way of speculative deduction. The metaphysical attributes of the world-ground are ethically barren. They furnish the possibility of an ethical nature, but they do not imply it as a necessity. There is no way, then, except to have immediate faith in our ideal of the perfect being, or else to appeal to experience to prove that the world-ground proceeds according to ethical principles. Our actual procedure is a mixture of both.

The empirical argument for the moral character of the world-ground is derived from our moral nature, the structure of society, and course of history. The two first are held to point to a moral author, and the last reveals a power not ourselves, making for righteousness, and hence moral.

§ 73. Our moral nature may be considered in two ways, (1) as an effect to be explained, and (2) in its immediate implications. The first problem, then, is to account for the existence of our moral nature.

The readiest solution is that this moral nature has a moral author. He that formed the eye, shall not he see? He that giveth man knowledge, shall not he know? So also, He that implanted in man an unalterable reverence for righteousness, shall not he himself be righteous? There can be no question about the knowledge of moral distinctions by the Creator. Such a doubt would imply that some knowledge is impossible to the source of all knowledge. The question can only concern his recognition of these distinctions in his action.

A great deal of ingenuity has been expended in trying to evade the conclusion from the moral effect to a moral cause. Much of this has been irrelevant, and all of it has been unsuccessful. As there is no known way of deducing intelligence from non-intelligence, so there is no known way of deducing the moral from the non-moral; except, of course, by the easy, but unsatisfactory, way of begging the question.

The irrelevance mentioned consists in the fact that a large part of this discussion has concerned itself with the inquiry how we come to recognize moral distinctions. This belongs to the debate between the empirical, and the intuitional school of morals, and does not necessarily touch the deeper question as to the reality of moral distinctions. To become relevant it must go on to claim that moral ideas are purely matters of opinion and prejudice, that, in fact, there is neither right nor wrong, and that one thing is as good and praiseworthy as another. Even this view has been theoretically affirmed, but it could never be practically maintained because of the sharp contradiction of life and conscience. The theorist himself could never maintain it outside of the closet. As soon as he came into contact with others he found himself compelled to acknowledge the difference of right and wrong. Hence spontaneous thought has generally regarded the moral nature in man as pointing to a moral character in God as its only sufficient ground. Speculation, too, knows of no better account to give.

§ 74. The moral nature, we said, may also be considered in its immediate implications. The claim has been made by a great many that conscience itself immediately testifies to a moral person over against us to whom it responds and to whom we are responsible. This claim can hardly be maintained in its literal form. In cases of high religious development and sensibility the feeling of obligation may take on this personal form. Right is the will of God; sin is sin against God. This view is both strongly asserted and warmly disputed; and, as is usual in such cases, there seems to be some truth on both sides. That conscience carries with it a direct assertion of God the judge and the avenger can hardly be pretended by any student of psychology; but that the assertion of a supreme judge and avenger has its chief roots in the moral nature cannot well be denied. The sacredness of right, the sin of oppression and injustice, the intolerable nature of a universe in which justice is not regarded, and guilt and innocence come to a common end—these considerations have led the race to posit a supreme justice and righteousness in the heavens. To this all literature bears witness; and practically these reflections are potent arguments. But in logic they are not arguments at all. To one who assumes nothing concerning the universe, one thing is no more surprising than another, and one thing is as allowable as another. If we do not assume that the universe is bound to be moral, we cannot be surprised at finding it non-moral. If we do not assume that our interests ought to be considered by the world-ground, we ought not to be astonished at finding them disregarded. The truth is that in arguments of this sort we have an underlying assumption of a perfect being, and of the supremacy of human and moral interests; and this gives the conclusion all its force. Suppose justice is not regarded, what does that prove unless we have assumed that justice must be regarded? Suppose the universe should turn out to be an ugly and shabby thing without moral or æsthetic value; who knows that it is bound to be the seat and manifestation of the true, the beautiful, and the good? The true force of such considerations is not logical; they serve rather and only to reveal to us the distressing and intolerable negations involved in certain views. Their rejection is not a logical inference, but an immediate refusal of the soul to abdicate its own nature and surrender to pessimism and despair. Hence whatever enriches the inner life strengthens the appropriate faith. A poem like "In Memoriam," a growing affection, a strong sense of justice, may do more for faith than acres of logic. But this insight into the true nature of the argument need not prevent us from yielding to it; for we have abundantly seen that it is the real basis of our whole mental life.

The considerations just dwelt upon are the gist of the so-called moral argument for the divine existence. We shall return to this point in the next chapter.

§ 75. The second form of empirical argument is drawn from the structure of life and society, and the course of history. Life itself is so constructed as to furnish a constant stimulus in moral directions. Nature itself inculcates with the utmost strenuousness the virtues of industry, prudence, foresight, self-control, honesty, truth, and helpfulness. In spite of the revised version, the way of the transgressor continues hard. When all allowance is made for failing cases, there can be no question that the nature of things is on the side of righteousness. This is so much the case that one school of moralists has claimed that the virtues are simply the great utilities. The possibility of such a claim shows the ethical framework of life. And it is true that the virtues are great utilities; ethical dispute could arise only over the claim that utilities are necessarily virtues;

and even then the debate would turn on the meaning of utility. If we define utility so as to include the satisfaction of the moral nature, there is no longer any ground of dispute.

Society, again, in its organized form is a moral institution with moral ends. However selfish individuals may be, they cannot live together without a social order which rests on moral ideas. And when these ideas are lacking, and injustice, oppression, and iniquity are enacted by law, social earthquakes and volcanoes begin to rock society to its foundations. The elements melt with fervent heat, and the heavens pass away with a great noise. Neither man nor society can escape the need of righteousness, truthfulness, honesty, purity, etc. No cunning, no power, can forever avail against the truth. No strength can long support a lie. The wicked may have great power and spread himself like a green bay-tree, but he passes away. The righteous are held in everlasting remembrance, but the name of the wicked rots. When wickedness is committed on a large scale by nations the result is even more marked. No lesson is more clearly taught by history than that righteousness exalteth a nation while sin is a reproach to any people. Nations rich in arts and sciences have perished, or been fearfully punished, because of evil-doing. Oppression, injustice, sensuality, have dragged nation after nation down into the dust and compelled them to drink the cup of a bitter and terrible retribution. The one truth, it is said, which can be verified concerning the world-ground is that it makes for righteousness.

§ 76. These empirical arguments, however, while they may serve to illustrate and confirm our faith, are plainly not its source. They all rest upon picked facts, and ignore some of the most prominent aspects of experience. This is especially the case with the historical argument. Here a scanty stream of progress is discovered; and the swamps and marshes of humanity through which it finds its doubtful way are overlooked. The area of progress is limited, while the great mass of humanity seems to have no significance for history or development, and to have no principle of movement above simple animal want. Here is no history, no progress, no ideas, only physical cravings and brute instincts. But we get on with the utmost cheer-

fulness by letting the "race" and "man" progress, and by ignoring individuals and men.
Clearly, we need something beside these facts
as the source of our faith. As in the world
we find marks of wisdom but not of perfect
wisdom; so in the world we find marks of
goodness but not of perfect goodness. In both
cases we pass from the limited wisdom and
goodness which we find to the perfect wisdom
and goodness in which we believe, only by force
of our faith in the perfect and complete ideal.
Then, having thus gained the conceptions, we
come back to the world of experience again
for their illustration. And the facts which
from a logical standpoint make a poor show as
proof are very effective as illustration; and this
passes for proof. It does indeed produce conviction; but the true nature of the argument
should not be overlooked. If any one had an
interest in maintaining the opposite hypotheses
of unwisdom and evil in the world-ground, a
great deal might be said for them. The great
mass of apparent insignificance and all the
facts of evil with which life is crowded would
lend themselves only too readily to illustrate
such a view. Of course a purely objective pro-

cedure would demand that we take all the facts into account and strike the average. Such a study of the facts would leave us in great uncertainty. Over against the good in nature we should put the evil; and this would hinder the affirmation of goodness. But over against the evil we should put the good; and this would not allow us to affirm a fundamental malignity. Over against the wisdom in nature we should put the meaningless aspects of existence, the cosmic labor which seems to end in nothing; and these would leave us in doubt whether we were not contemplating the work of some blind demiurge rather than of supreme wisdom. But over against these facts we should put the ever-growing rational wonder of the universe; and this would drive us into doubt again. The outcome would probably be the affirmation of a being either morally indifferent, or morally imperfect, or morally good, but limited by some insuperable necessity which forbids anything better than our rather shabby universe.

But the mind is not satisfied to take this road. It will not allow its ideals to collapse without some effort to save them. It prefers rather to maintain its faith in the ideal, and to set aside the conflicting facts as something not yet understood, but which to perfect insight would fall into harmony. This assumption is made both in the cognitive and the moral realm; and, so far as logic goes, it is as well-founded in one realm as in the other. In both cases our procedure is not due to any logical compulsion; it is rather an act of instinctive self-defence on the part of the mind whereby it seeks to save its life from destruction.

§ 77. That experience does not prove the goodness of the world-ground is generally allowed. The claim of the optimist is rather that experience is not incompatible therewith; and the opposing claim of the pessimist is that our optimistic faith must perish when confronted with the dark realities of life and nature. A word of exposition seems desirable, as both parties have done not a little fighting in the dark.

The pessimistic conclusion from the apparent worthlessness and insignificance of existence to the denial of creative wisdom, as distinct from mere skill, rests upon two assumptions: (1) that perfect wisdom is compatible only with a perfect work; and (2) that we know the facts in question to be truly worthless and insignificant. In the first assumption we detect only a certain pharisaism of the intellect; and in the second we detect an arrogance which is not entirely compatible with the humility which so often renounces knowledge altogether. The pessimist may say that he proceeds inductively, and that where he sees no purpose he affirms none; but in this he rather deludes himself. Where he sees no purpose he denies purpose; where he sees no significance he denies significance. This denial must be recalled; and the optimist and pessimist must choose sides. The optimist says that he finds wisdom as far as he can understand, and he knows his own insight to be very limited. He prefers, therefore, to believe that advancing knowledge will dispel our difficulties. He adds that this is the method on which thought generally proceeds. Thus experience is largely chaotic. A reign of law is discerned only to a very limited extent. But instead of suffering chaos to dispute the sovereignty of law we rule it out as an intolerable and impossible thought. The optimistic faith is only another case of the same principle, and is certainly as respectable as

15

the pessimistic faith which is based on the assumption of omniscence.

But this is only a skirmish; we must, if possible, come to closer quarters. The debate has generally been confused by introducing the superlative notion of the best possible system; and this has given rise to limitless verbal quibbling. This notion has no clear content, and taken quantitatively it is a contradiction, like the largest possible number or the largest possible limited space. But if we take the notion qualitatively, it must still contain quantitative factors, and the difficulty reappears. The notion, then, is to be dismissed. Of any finite system whatever the questions would be possible: Why thus and not otherwise? Why now and not then? Why on this plane and not on that? Why so much and not more or less? Questions of this sort are forever possible and forever insoluble, and should be sacredly left to debating youths and other transcendent intelligences. The only question that has any meaning is whether the system is good or not.

§ 78. The optimist claims that the system is good, the pessimist claims that it is bad. But plainly no judgment can be reached unless we have a knowledge of the system as a whole and especially a knowledge of its outcome. A careful logic would dismiss the suit on the ground of no jurisdiction. But as the litigants insist on being heard, we must continue to follow the case.

The present type of thought in the speculative world is somewhat favorable to optimism. The current notions of development, progress, and improvement enable the optimist to claim that everything shows a tendency to the better. The universe is not yet complete, but only in its raw beginnings. Meanwhile we see, if not a finished optimism, at least a decided meliorism, and meliorism is optimism. He calls, therefore, upon the pessimist to master the significance of the great law of evolution, and pending this mastery to hold his peace. The pessimist wants to know why things were not made perfect at once; but the current type of thought declines the question as a survival of an obsolete mode of thought. If evolution is the law of life, of course the present must seem imperfect relative to the future, and the past imperfect relative to the present. This is fairly good chaffing, but it does not meet the question why this progress might not have been accomplished at less cost of toil and struggle and pain. In truth, it is only another way of saying that the system is to be judged only in its outcome and the outcome is assumed to be good. The fancy that evolution in any way diminishes the Creator's responsibility for evil is really somewhat infantile. It rests on the assumption that there is some element of chance or self-determination in the system whereby it is able to make new departures on its own account. But in a mechanical system there is no such element, and the founder is responsible for the outcome.

It is also worth while to note how completely the discussion rests upon the assumed supremacy of human interests. What is meant by a good or a bad universe? Implicitly our interests furnish the standard. That universe is good which meets our wishes, and that is bad which ignores them. But how do we know that the universe exists for us? May it not well have inscrutable ends which it perfectly realizes, and may not our complaints be like those of a nest of ants who should first assume that the universe is meant to be an ant-hill, and should then condemn it for its unhappy adjustment to formic necessities? Pessimism is the most striking illustration possible of the fact that the mind is bound to measure the universe by itself.

But once again, what do we mean by a good or bad universe, and how is such goodness or badness to be tested? Here the debaters have generally imposed upon themselves with abstractions. The pessimist is apt to forget that pain in the abstract is nothing, and that it has existence only as felt by sensitive beings. He heaps up all the misery of all beings, past, present and future, and forthwith makes a sum so great as to hide all well-being from his vision. Thus he resembles the man who, from long dwelling in the hospital, should heap up in one thought all the sickness of the world, and should become so impressed thereby as to conclude that health and soundness nowhere exist. The illusion is completed by attributing this sum of pains to the abstraction, man; and then all the conditions for profound closet woe and the appropriate rhetoric are fully met. But if we are to get on we must dismiss this integral of abstract pains and this abstract man who suffers them, and ask for living men to come forward and testify. The abstract man cannot be miserable, but only concrete, conscious men. The declaration that the world is bad must, then, mean that its structure is such as necessarily to make life not worth living. The question, then, becomes simply one as to the worth of life. This question each person must decide for himself. The vanity of argument is apparent. As well might one appeal to theory to decide whether he enjoys his dinner. The spectacle of a closet philosopher deciding by theorizing whether life is worth living, might move one either to mirth or to compassion, according to one's mood or nature.

§ 79. The value of life must be decided by the race; and the race has never recognized the pessimist's standard of value. This has commonly been taken from the passive sensibility; as if the only good in life were passive pleasure, and the only evil passive pain. Hence the pessimist has often demanded why this passive pleasure is not incessantly produced without effort of our own. A being of infinite goodness might do it just as well as not; and the failure to do so weighs heavily upon our so-called minds. But experience shows two sets of values, those of the passive, and those of our active nature, and the race has agreed in placing all significant values of life in the latter class, and in viewing the former with a certain measure of contempt. Conscious self-development, growing self-possession, progress, conquest, the successful putting forth of energy and the resulting growth—these are the things which the race has judged truly valuable. The mere presence of pain has seldom shaken the faith of any one except the sleek and well-fed speculator. The couch of suffering is more often the scene of loving trust than are the pillows of luxury and the chief seats at feasts. The human soul, as long as it retains anything noble and reverend in its nature, is amazingly loyal to faith in supreme goodness. The real difficulty for the race has never been the fact of passive pain, but the apparent moral indifference which the cosmos often shows; and this difficulty it has provided for by assuming a future adjustment of all rights and wrongs.

But assuming that life is not worth living, the question arises, Who or what is to blame? In

deciding this we should need to distinguish between the evil which arises necessarily from
the structure of the cosmos and that which is
due to our own folly and sin. The latter cannot be laid to the account of the universe except in a roundabout way. We may complain
of the system for making our folly possible,
but the complaint will not weigh much with
the upright mind and conscience. A large part
of our worst woes are of our own making.
The most fearful ills of life result from laws in
themselves good, such as the law of heredity,
of social solidarity, and mutual dependence.

In the animal world the problem of evil is
simply one of pain. The extent and nature of
animal pain are entirely unknown. A multitude of facts indicate that even the more highly
organized animals are far less sensitive to pain
than men are; while of the sensibility of the
simple organic forms we have no knowledge
whatever.

§ 80. Proper pessimism is even more illogical
than optimism. There is evil, but there is also
good in the universe. There is pain, but there
is also happiness. Pain results from animal

structure, but only as an implication, not as a manifest aim.   The evolutionists have often pointed out that the tendency of life must be to increase pleasure and eliminate pain.   For pain that exists the optimist often succeeds in showing a beneficent function.   The high ministries of pain in the development of the virtues and graces of character are a favorite theme with the moralist and the preacher.   Hence thoughtful pessimists, as distinct from the rhetorical shrieker, have generally concluded not to malignity, but to a limited or conditioned goodness.   Why might not pain have been dispensed with as a means?   Why might not everything have been made perfect at once?   Things may be as good as possible, but if there be an omnipotent goodness at the root of things, why are they not better?   There is no end to these questions, and also no answer.   The solution of the problem demands data which lie beyond our horizon.   The desultory character of the actual debate is evident.   It is a series of skirmishes between armies in a fog, and ends mostly in noise and panic.   At last we have to choose sides.   We may say that there is some inscrutable necessity which prevents

things from getting on faster and better than
they do; or we may hold to the moral and metaphysical perfection of the world - ground and
believe in a possible solution which at present
we do not comprehend. The facts neither compel nor forbid this faith. They permit it, and
to some extent illustrate it; and the mind, with
that faith in the perfect ideal which underlies
all its operations, refuses to stop short of the
highest.

§ 81. Only a reference is necessary to the
various theories of the origin and meaning of
evil. A first thought, of course, was to find
its source in something altogether apart from
God. A devil, a self-existent evil principle, an
intractable matter, or something of the sort,
was adduced in explanation. When advancing thought showed the untenability of such a
view, recourse was generally had to the notion
that the eternal truths, or necessities of reason,
are in some way responsible for evil. Unfortunately no one ever succeeded in connecting
the eternal truths with the particular facts of
evil. No one ever showed that any eternal
truth would have been violated, or that any

other damage would have been done, if many of the obnoxious features of the cosmic order had been left out. Many have also taken great comfort in the thought of evil as a necessary means to good. It is the shadow which brings out the light, the discord which heightens the sense of harmony. It is, too, a pedagogical factor in the development of humanity. Such considerations have given birth to limitless fine writing and served to give the appearance of logic and philosophy to a purely practical postulate. In themselves they are so inadequate to a complete solution of the problem that they aggravate rather than relieve the case; and in so far they become a part of the problem itself.

§ 82. Speculative theology has produced elaborate schemes of the ethical attributes as well as of the metaphysical. Love, mercy, justice, righteousness, and holiness have been set up as separate attributes; and a good deal of ingenuity has been shown in adjusting their relations. Into these questions we have no need to enter. The ethical nature of God is sufficiently determined for all religious, and, we may add, for all speculative purposes, as being holy love. These factors belong together. Love without holiness would be simply well-wishing without any ethical content; and holiness without love would be a lifeless negation.

Love needs no definition; but the notion of holiness is not so clear. Negatively, holiness implies the absence of all tendencies to evil and of all delight in evil. Positively, it involves the delight in and devotion to goodness. The knowledge of evil must exist in the divine thought, but perfect holiness implies that it finds no echo in the divine sensibility and no realization in the divine will. It further implies, positively, that in God the ideal of moral perfection is realized; and this ideal involves love as one of its chief factors.

In determining this ideal we can only fall back upon the immediate testimony of the moral nature. No legislation can make anything an abiding part of this ideal unless it be commanded by conscience; and nothing can be allowed to enter into it which is forbidden by conscience. It is this voice of conscience which distinguishes the non-moral good and evil of simple sensibility from the moral good and evil of the ethical life.

§ 83. In maintaining the absoluteness of God as a moral being a curious difficulty arises from the nature of the moral life itself. This life implies community and has no meaning for the absolutely single and only. Love without an object is nothing. Justice has no meaning except between persons. Benevolence is impossible without plurality and community. Hence, if we conceive God as single and alone, we must say that, as such, he is only potentially a moral being. To pass from potential to actual moral existence the Infinite must have an object.

Several ways out of this difficulty offer themselves. First, we may admit that the absolute and essential God is metaphysical only and not moral. His morality is but an incident of his cosmic activity, and not something pertaining to his own essential existence. God's metaphysical existence is absolute, but his moral life is relative to creation and has no meaning or possibility apart from it.

The immediate implication of this view is another, as follows: God is not absolute and self-sufficient in his ethical life, but needs the presence of the finite in order to realize his own ethical potentialities and attain to a truly

moral existence. But this view either makes
God dependent on the world for his own complete self - realization or it makes the cosmic
activity the necessary means by which God
comes into full self-possession. In either form
the moral is made subordinate to the metaphysical, the proper absoluteness of God is denied, and a strong tendency to pantheism appears. When the view is made to affirm, as
often happens, that God apart from the world
is as impossible as the world apart from God,
we have pronounced pantheism.

The third view aims to escape these difficulties by providing for community of personal
life in the divine unity itself. In this way the
conditions of ethical life are found within the
divine nature; and the ethical absoluteness of
God is assured. But how this community in
unity is possible is one of the deepest mysteries
of speculation. The only suggestion of solution seems to lie in the notion of necessary
creation. Such creation would be unbegun and
endless, and would depend on the divine nature
and not on the divine will. If now we suppose
the divine nature to be such that the essential
God must always and eternally produce other

beings than himself, those other beings, though numerically distinct from himself, would be essential implications of himself. There would be at once a numerical plurality and an organic unity. Hence pantheism, while viewing God and the world as numerically distinct, has always maintained that they are organically and essentially one. Such a conception can in no way be discredited by a verbal shuffling of formal ideas such as one and many, unity and plurality. Formally these ideas are opposed; but reality has ways of uniting our formal oppositions in indivisible syntheses which our formal thought cannot construe.

But we have already seen that we cannot carry the actual world of finite things into God without speculative disaster and shipwreck. It only remains to abandon the notion of a necessary creation whereby God forever posits community for himself, or else to find its objects apart from the finite system as persons coeternal with God himself. If it be said that this is polytheism, the answer would be that polytheism implies a plurality of mutually independent beings. If it be said that these dependent personalities are created, the answer would be that their existence does not depend on the divine will, but on the divine nature. They, therefore, coexist with God; nor could God exist without them. If, then, in pantheism we say that the world is God, what can we say of these but that they are God, at once numerically distinct and organically one? If creation seems to be an expression implying will, we may exchange it for the profoundly subtle terms of early theological speculation, and speak of an eternal generation and procession. These terms throw no light upon the matter, and only serve to mark off the eternal implications of the divine nature from the free determinations of the divine will.

The consideration of the ethical absoluteness of God has led us into speculations which suggest the Christian doctrine of the Trinity, and which may explain why so many thinkers have insisted on holding that doctrine in spite of the formal opposition of the ideas of unity and trinity. But into this question we have no call to enter. In any case speculation can only call attention to difficulties and suggest possibilities without being able to say anything positive.

CHAPTER VII.

THEISM AND LIFE.

The considerations thus far dwelt upon are chiefly such as address themselves to man as a contemplative being. But man is not merely nor mainly contemplation, he is also will and action. He must, then, have something to work for, aims to realize, and ideals by which to live. In real life the centre of gravity of theistic faith lies in its relation to these aims and ideals. God is seen to be that without which our ideals collapse or are made unattainable, and the springs of action are broken. Hence the existence of God is affirmed not on speculative or theoretical grounds, but because of the needs of practical life. This has often been called the moral argument for the divine existence; a better name would be the practical argument.

§ 84. That this argument has no logical value is evident. It is essentially a conclusion from

16

what we think ought to be to what is, or from our subjective interests to objective fact; and such a conclusion is forever invalid in logic. It becomes valid only on the assumption, expressed or implicit, that what our nature calls for, reality must, in one form or another, supply. Hence Kant, who was one of the leading expounders of this conception, expressly denied its speculative cogency. On the contrary, he claimed to have shown that, by way of speculation, neither proof nor disproof is possible; and in this balance of the speculative reason practical interests may be allowed to turn the scale. All that can be done, then, is to show that theism is a demand of our moral nature, a necessity of practical life. Whether to accept this subjective necessity as the warrant for the objective fact every one must decide for himself. That our entire mental life rests upon such an acceptance we have already abundantly seen.

The moral argument has often been mismanaged. Sometimes it is put forward as proof, and then it falls an easy prey to the hostile critic. Again, the discussion has often taken on a hedonistic turn and run off into gross selfishness, by the side of which even atheism itself might seem morally superior. We need, then, to consider the relation of theism and atheism to the moral life.

§ 85. A peremptory rejection of atheism as destructive of all moral theory might not be unwarranted, but it would fail to show the real points of difficulty. To do this we need to consider the matter more in detail. Any system of practical ethics involves several distinct factors: (1) a set of formal moral judgments concerning right and wrong, (2) a set of aims or ideals to be realized, and (3) a set of commands to be obeyed. In the first class we have only the moral form of conduct; in the second class we have the material contents of conduct, and in the third class the contents of the two first are prescribed as duties. The perennial short-coming of traditional ethics has been the failure to see the equal necessity of all of these factors. The result has been numberless one-sided systems with resulting war and confusion.

What, now, is the bearing of atheism upon these several factors, the system of judgments, the system of ideals, the system of duties? We consider the last first.

To answer this question we must consider the automatism involved in atheism. This implication, though not perhaps strictly necessary, can be escaped only by admissions fatal to all thinking, and hence atheism and automatism have generally been united. Hence when we begin to construct a system of duties we are met at once by the question how an automaton can have duties. To this question there is no answer. The traditional evasion consists in saying that moral judgments, like æsthetic judgments, are independent of the question of freedom. In determining what is beautiful or ugly we take no account of freedom or necessity, and the same is true in determining what is right or wrong. If ethics were only a set of moral judgments, this claim would not be without some foundation. But ethics is also a set of precepts to be obeyed, and obedience is reckoned as merit, and disobedience as demerit; and for these notions the conception of freedom is absolutely necessary.

The same evasion sometimes takes on another form, as follows: We judge persons for what they are, no matter how they became so. A thing which is ugly by necessity is still ugly, and a person who is wicked by necessity is still wicked.

It is, then, a mistake to claim that our judgment of persons is in any way conditioned by belief in their freedom. To this the answer is that our judgments of persons are from a double standpoint, that of perfection and that of ability. On the former depend judgments of imperfection, on the latter depend judgments of guilt or innocence. But however imperfect one may be, he cannot be responsible for anything that transcends his ability. So, then, in any atheistic system the question must still remain, How can automata have duties? This question is so important that it is much to be wished that the universal necessity or some of its subordinate phases might be brought to consider it. If this question were once answered, it would next be in order to inquire how an automaton could perform its duties if necessity set in another direction, or how it could help performing them if necessity set that way. Another interesting and important question would concern the ground of the moral difference between the several automata. These questions, however, are not likely to receive a speedy answer, owing, of course, to the intractability and illogicality of the cosmic necessity in general; and we shall do better to go on to consider the bearing of atheism upon ethics as a system of moral judgments.

§ 86. Our formal judgments of right and wrong have no direct dependence upon theistic faith. It is at this point that the moral argument has been most mismanaged. How can the obligation of justice, truth, benevolence, gratitude be made to depend even on the existence of God? And with what face can we pretend that atheism would make these virtues less binding than they are? These are absolute moral intuitions. If no one regarded them they would still be valid. Certainly if they depend at all on theism it must be indirectly. In this respect our moral judgments are like our judgments of true and false. The rejection of theism would not make the unjust just any more than it would make the false true. But in both cases we can show that our nature falls into discord with itself, or is unable to defend itself against scepticism, until our thought reaches the conception of God as supreme reason and holy will. Then reason and conscience, from being psychological facts in us, become universal cosmic laws, and their supremacy is assured. But so long as they are limited to human and terrestrial manifestation they are perpetually open to the sceptical surmise that after all they may only be our way of thinking, and hence matters of opinion. That this conclusion has been persistently drawn from atheistic premises is a matter of history. This is further strengthened by the fact that right and wrong, if distinct, can have no application to actual life because of the universal automatism. On this account theorists of this school have generally tended to reduce the distinction to one of utility and inutility. This distinction plainly exists; and by and by we remember that right and wrong are other names for the same thing. Forthwith we use them, and thus give variety to our terminology and save moral distinctions at the same time.

§ 87. A consistent atheism, then, cannot defend itself against ethical scepticism any more than against speculative scepticism in general. But there is no need to insist upon this point; for if these formal principles were set on high above all doubt, we should still not have all the conditions of a complete moral system. Such a system involves, not only these formal principles, but also a set of extra-ethical conceptions which condition their application. Of these the most important are our general world-view, our conception of life, its meaning and destiny, our conception of personality also, and its essential sacredness. These elements, however, express no immediate intuition of conscience, but are taken from our general theory of things. Yet any variation in these elements must lead to corresponding variations in practice, even while the formal principles remain the same.

Illustrations abound. The law of benevolence may be absolute as a disposition, but its practical application is limited by a prudent self-regard on the one hand, and by our conception of the nature and significance of the object on the other. Only a high conception of humanity gives sacredness to human rights and incites to strenuous effort in its behalf. The golden rule, also, must be conditioned by some conception of the true order and dignity of life; otherwise it might be perfectly obeyed in a world of sots and gluttons. With Plato's conception of the relation of the individual to society, Plato's doctrine of infanticide seems correct enough. With Aristotle's theory of man and his destiny, Aristotle's

theory of slavery is altogether defensible. From
the standpoint of the ancient ethnic conceptions,
the accompanying ethnic morality was entirely
allowable. Apart from some conception of the
sacredness of personality, it is far from sure that
the redemption of society could not be more
readily reached by killing off the idle and mis-
chievous classes than by philanthropic effort for
their improvement. And Christianity wrought
its great moral revolution, not by introducing
new moral principles, but by revealing new conceptions of God and man and their mutual relations. By making all men the children of a
common Father it did away with the earlier ethnic conceptions and the barbarous morality based
upon them. By making every man the heir of
eternal life it gave to him a sacredness which
he could never lose and which might never be
ignored. By making the moral law the expression of a Holy Will, it brought that law out of
its impersonal abstraction and assured its ultimate triumph. Moral principles may be what
they were before, but moral practice is forever
different. Even the earth itself has another look
now that it has a heaven above it.

These illustrations show that the actual guidance of life involves not only a knowledge of formal moral principles, but also a series of extramoral conceptions which condition their application. They also show how impossible it is to construct a code of conduct which shall be independent of our general theory of things.

Oversight of this fact has been the perennial weakness of the intuitional ethics. It has dreaded to take the aim and outcome of conduct into account lest it fall into utilitarianism. As a result it has had to fall back upon purely formal principles which, while good and even necessary as far as they go, furnish no positive guidance for practical life. We are told to be virtuous, to be conscientious, to act from right motives, and to act so that the maxims of our conduct shall be fit to be universal law. But this only concerns the form of conduct and overlooks the fact that conduct must have aims beyond itself, and that these aims must be in harmony with the nature of things. Besides, it is narrow. The moral task of the individual by no means consists solely in being conscientious or even virtuous, but rather and chiefly in an objective realization of the good. Mere conscientiousness is the narrowest possible conception of virtue, and the lowest possible aim. A worthy moral aim can be found only in the thought of a kingdom of righteousness and blessedness realized in a community of moral persons. But no one can work with this aim without implicitly assuming a higher power, which is the guarantee of the possibility of its realization. In other words, morality which goes beyond mere conscientiousness must have recourse to religion.

§ 88. Working ethics must present not only rules for conduct, but ideals to realize; and here we touch the point of chief practical difficulty with all ethics. The great practical trouble, after all, is less a lack of light than a general discouragement, a doubt whether anything worth while is attainable. We can, indeed, live in peace and mutual helpfulness with our neighbors without looking beyond visible existence; but when we are looking for some supreme aim which shall give meaning and dignity to life and make it worth while to live, forthwith we begin to grope. We can see with some clearness what ought to be, but we are not so sure that what ought to be is. Moral ideals are fair, no doubt, but it is not so clear that they are practicable. Life is short.

The great cosmic order is not manifestly constructed for moral ends. It seems mostly indifferent to them, and at times even opposed. It
only remains that we find the law of life within
the sphere of visible existence. And here too
ideals do not count for much. Virtue within
the limits of prudence is wise, but an *abandon*
of goodness is hardly worldly-wise. Upon the
whole, visible life seems not over-favorable to
ideals, unless it be the modest one of not being
righteous overmuch. One could indeed wish it
were otherwise, that virtue were at home in the
universe and that our ideals were only shadows
of the glorious reality. But what avails it to
wish? It is not so, and we must make the best
of it. To meet the depressing and disheartin-
ing influences arising from considerations of
this kind the race has always had recourse to
the belief in God and the future life. Visible
existence is not all, and righteousness is at the
heart of things. Hence we may believe in its
final triumph, and in some new existence we
shall see it. This practical conviction must be
shared by the theorist to this extent: either
we must restrict our ideals to those attainable
in our present life, or we must enlarge the life

so as to make the larger ideals attainable and save them from collapse. The first duty of even a theory of morals is to be rational; and it can never be rational to live for the impossible. Our conception of the nature and destiny of a being must determine our conception of the law the being ought to follow.

Some have affected to find an unholy selfishness in this claim, and have even dreaded to admit a future life lest the purity of their devotion should be sullied. This is one of the drollest whimseys which our self-sophisticated time has produced. But since this pure devotion is mostly manifested in polemics, there is room for suspecting that it is mainly rhetorical virtue. In this respect it seems to be about on a par with the delicate feeling of the biblical critic, who with his mouth full of beef or mutton professes to be shocked at the cruelty to animals involved in the temple sacrifices. But, however that may be, the feeling, so far as it is real and not professional, rests upon an inability to distinguish between a demand that we be paid for our virtue, and the revolt of our nature against a system which treats good and bad alike, and throws the better half of our nature back upon itself as absurd and meaningless. Neither God nor the future life is needed to pay us for present virtue, but rather as the conditions without which our nature falls into irreconcilable discord with itself and passes on to pessimism and despair. High and continued effort is impossible without correspondingly high and abiding hopes. Moral theory which looks to form only and ignores ends reduces conduct to etiquette. It may claim, indeed, to be sublime, but it misses sublimity by just one fatal step.

§ 89. The only elements in ethics that can claim to be absolute are purely formal, and furnish only a negative guidance for life. All working theories of ethics must transcend these formal principles, and seek for the supreme moral aims and ideals in some general theory of life and the world. This leads us to consider the third factor mentioned as involved in ethical system. What is the relation of atheism to the ideals of conduct, or what ideals can atheism furnish?

This question is sufficiently answered by a moment's survey of life from the standpoint of atheistic theory. To begin with, we have a blind power, or set of powers, perpetually energizing without purpose or plan, without self-knowledge or objective knowledge, forever weaving and forever unweaving because of some inscrutable necessity. The outcome is, among innumerable other things, a serio - comic procession of " cunning casts in clay" in all forms from mollusk to man. No one of these forms means any more than any other, for nothing *means* anything in this theory. A procession of wax figures would not be more truly automatic than these forms are in all respects. When we come to the human forms we find a curious set of illusions. Most of them necessarily believe in a God, whereas there is no God. Most of them necessarily believe that they are free, whereas they are not free. Most of them necessarily believe themselves responsible, whereas no one and nothing is responsible. Most of them necessarily believe in a distinction between right and wrong, whereas there is no distinction. Most of them necessarily believe in duty, whereas automata cannot have duties, or cannot perform them, or cannot help performing them, according as necessity determines. All of them, without exception, necessarily assume the possibility of logical thought and reasoning, whereas this assumption is totally unfounded. Further, the members of this procession are perpetually falling out, and that is the end of them as individuals. For a time the melancholy order is kept up by the fundamental unconsciousness through the incessant reproduction of new forms; but there are signs that the process itself will yet come to an end, and leave no sign. Such is the history, meaning, and outcome of human life on atheistic theory. It seems needless to add anything about the moral ideals of atheism. If we speak of them at all it is only by a fundamental inconsistency which, however, is not to be reckoned to ourselves, but to the basal necessity, which is given to doing odd things.

The difficulties of atheism in constructing a system of ethics may be summed up as follows :

First, ethics as a system of duties is absurd in a system of automatism. The attendant ideas of obligation and responsibility, merit and demerit, guilt and innocence, are illusory in such a theory. Second, ethics as a system of judgments concerning right and wrong is in unstable equilibrium in atheistic theory. For atheism has no way of escaping the sceptical implications of all systems of necessity. The necessity of denying proper moral differences among persons empties our moral judgments of all application to practical life. Third, atheism can hold out no good for the individual or for the race but annihilation. At each of these points Christian theism is adequate. By affirming a free Creator and free creatures it gives moral government a meaning. By making the moral nature of man the manifestation of an omnipotent and eternal righteousness which underlies the cosmos, it sets our moral convictions above all doubt and overthrow. Finally, it provides a conception of man and his destiny which gives man a worthy task and an inalienable sacredness. The mere etiquette of conscientiousness is transformed into loyal devotion to the law and kingdom of God.

§ 90. The attitude of atheistic speculation towards religion has undergone a great change in recent years. From an atheistic standpoint this would mean that the basal and unconscious necessity is producing a new order of conceptions. At all events, the sturdy brutalities of the last century are out of date. The ancient claim that

17

religion is an adventitious accretion without any essential foundation in human nature is obsolescent if not obsolete. The religious nature is recognized as a universal human fact, and as one which cannot be ignored. The natural assumption in such a case would be that the objective implications of this fact should be recognized as real, at least until they are positively disproved. Failing to do this, we have an instinct without an object, an organ without a function, a demand with no supply. This is the position of the religious nature in modern atheistic systems. They cannot get along without it, and are utterly at a loss to get along with it. The need of making some provision for religion without admitting its objective foundation has caused infinite embarrassment and given birth to many schemes for its removal. In the lack of God we have been urged to worship the cosmos; and "cosmic emotion" has been put forward as something to take the place of religion. Some have emphasized the claims of the sun as a religious object, seeing that it is the source of light and warmth and life. Humanity, also, has been set up as a supreme object of worship and endowed with many extraordinary functions and attributes. The Unknowable, too, has its altar, and has been worshipped with much emotion, mainly of the cosmic sort. Occasionally a suspicion seems to come across the minds of the apostles that these shreds and tatters of old idolatries hardly satisfy the religious nature, but they drive it off by sharply reminding us that we cannot have everything we want. As death ends all for the individual, much attention has been devoted to proclaiming the selfishness of the desire for a future life. In what respect it is more selfish to desire to live hereafter than it is to desire to live to-morrow has never been clearly pointed out. To fill up the gap left by the vanishing of the immortal hope a somewhat blind enthusiasm for progress has been invoked. The meaning or value of a progress whose subjects are perpetually perishing is somewhat doubtful; but this fact is covered up by invoking the fiction " Humanity " earnestly and repeatedly. This device, however, is losing its efficacy, and the cant of progress is receding. From a purely inductive standpoint, the actual man is a poor affair at best; and it is doubtful if he will ever amount to much. We know more and appear better than past generations, but it is not clear that character is much superior. The æsthetics of life progress and material comfort increases; but these things do not necessarily involve a corresponding moral progress. And anyhow the notion of indefinite progress for humanity upon the earth is distinctly forbidden by the conditions of physical existence. Both progress and posterity bid fair to come to an end. And then for the race, as now for the individual, the whole meaningless stir of existence will have sunk back into silence and left no trace or sign. And this is the end, this the outcome of the "high intuition," this the result of the "grand progress which is bearing Humanity onward to a higher intelligence and a nobler character." In such a view there is no healing and no inspiration. It is in unstable equilibrium and must either return towards theism, or pass on to pessimism and despair.

The contention of this chapter was not that God exists, but rather that theistic faith is such an implication of our moral nature and practical life that atheism must tend to wreck both life and conscience. That contention has been established.

CONCLUSION.

In the Introduction it was pointed out that thought demands some things, forbids some things, and permits some things. The first class must be accepted, for it consists of the laws and categories of reason and their implications. The second class must be rejected, as it violates the nature of reason. The third class belongs to the great realm of probability and practical life. In this realm we reach conclusions, not by logical demonstration, but by a weighing of probabilities, or by a consideration of practical needs, or by a taking for granted in the interest of ideal tendencies. In this realm belief, or assent, involves an element of volition. Logic leaves us in uncertainty, and the will comes in to overturn the speculative equilibrium and precipitate the conclusion.

We have abundantly seen that theistic faith has its root in all of these realms, and cannot dispense with any of them. Each contributes

something of value. The speculative intellect
necessarily stops short of the religious idea of
God, but it gives us some fundamental elements of the conception. It is, too, of the
highest service in outlining the general form
which the theistic conception must take in order to be consistent with itself and the laws
of thought. Here speculation performs the
invaluable negative service of warding off a
multitude of misconceptions, especially of a
pantheistic type, which have been morally as
pernicious in history as they are speculatively
absurd. But a mind with only cognitive interests would find no occasion to consider more
than the metaphysical attributes of God. The
demand to consider God as having ethical and
æsthetic attributes arises not from the pure intellect, but from the moral and æsthetic nature.
Here the understanding has only the negative
function of maintaining consistency and pre-
venting collision with the laws of thought.
The positive content of these attributes cannot
be learned from logic, and the faith in their
objective reality must at last rest on our immediate conviction that the universe is no more
the abode of the true than it is of the beauti-

ful and the good. Indeed, the true itself, except as truth of fact, is a purely ideal element, and derives all its significance from its connection with the beautiful and the good. For truth of fact has only a utilitarian value apart from the nature of the fact that is true. If the universe were only a set of facts—such as, Water boils at 100° C.—it would have nothing in it to awaken wonder, enthusiasm, and reverence; and "cosmic emotion" would be quite as much out of place as religious sentiment.

Logically considered, our entire mental life rests upon a fallacy of the form known as the illicit process; in other words, our conclusions are too large for the premises. A set of ideals arises in the mind under the stimulus of experience, but not as transcripts of experience. These ideals implicitly determine our mental procedure, and they do it all the more surely because we are generally unconscious of them. Our so-called proofs consist, not in deducing them from experience, but in illustrating them by experience. The facts which make against the ideal are set aside as problems not yet understood. In this way we maintain our conception of a rational universe, or of a God of perfect wisdom and goodness. We illustrate by picked facts, and this passes for proof. Of course it is not proof, but only an illustration of pre-existing conceptions.

Logic, then, is in its full right in pointing out the non-demonstrative character of these arguments, but it is miserably narrow when it fails to see that these undemonstrated ideals are still the real foundation of our mental life. Without implicit faith in them no step can be taken in any field. The mind as a whole, then, is in its full right when, so long as these ideals are not positively disproved, it accepts them on its own warrant and works them out into the rich and ever-growing conquests of our modern life. By the side of this great faith and its great results the formal objections of formal logic sink almost into a despicable impertinence.

Of all these ideals that rule our life theism is the sum and source. The cognitive ideal of the universe, as a manifestation of the Supreme Reason, leads to theism. The moral ideal of the universe, as a manifestation of the Supreme Righteousness, leads to theism. The practical ideal of a "far-off divine event to which the whole creation moves" leads to theism. In short, while theism is demonstrated by nothing, it is implicit in everything. It cannot be proved without begging the question, or denied without ending in absurdity.

Poor atheism, on the other hand, first puts out its eyes by its primal unfaith in the truth of our nature and of the system of things, and then proceeds to make a great many flourishes about "reason," "science," "progress," and the like, in melancholy ignorance of the fact that it has made all these impossible. If consistent thinking were still possible one could not help feeling affronted by a theory which violates the conditions of all thinking and theorizing. It is an outlaw by its own act, yet insolently demands the protection of the laws it seeks to overthrow. Supposing logical thought possible, there seems to be no escape from regarding atheism as a pathological compound of ignorance and insolence. On the one hand, there is a complete ignorance of all the implications of valid knowing, and on the other a ludicrous identification of itself with science. Its theory of knowledge is picked up ready-made among the crudities of spontaneous thought, and when the self-destructive implications of atheism are pointed out, in-

stead of justifying itself from its own premises,
it falls back on thoughtless common-sense, which
forthwith rejects the implications.   Of course
the question is not whether the implications be
true or false, but whether they be implications.
This point is happily ignored, and the defence
is complete.   It only remains to pick some flaws
in theistic argument, and to skirmish a little with
" the vastness of the Possible," and atheism may
be regarded as established.   To be sure, there is
no mental health or insight furnished by the
doctrine.   It must proclaim our entire nature
misleading.   The universe which has evolved the
human mind as the " correspondence of inner relations to outer relations" has produced a strange
non-correspondence here.   The all-illuminating
formula, It is because it must be, sheds only
a feeble light.   The conception of blind power
working for apparent ends, of non-intelligence
producing intelligence, of unconsciousness producing consciousness, of necessity producing
ideas of freedom and duty—this conception is
not a transparent one.   But these considerations
avail nothing.   The nightmare of the " Possible" is upon the speculator and prevents the
proper working of intelligence.   Under the spell,

the " Probable " and the " Rational " are entirely
lost sight of.   The state is pathologic, and belongs to the mental pathologist rather than the
philosopher.

Considering atheistic procedure as a whole, an
ill-conditioned mind might lose patience with it;
but there is no occasion for warmth, for according to the theory itself, logical thought is not
possible.   Thoughts come and go, not according
to any inherent rationality, but as produced by
necessity.   This probably contains the explanation of some of the extraordinary logic of atheistic treatises.   Any hiatus between premises
and conclusion is due to necessity.   Any strange
backwardness in drawing a manifest conclusion
has the same cause.   All lapses into sentiment
just when logic is called for are equally necessary.   Even the mistakes of theism and the hard-
ness and uncircumcision of the critical heart
have an equally solid foundation.   A great authority, speaking of the advanced thinker, says,
" He, like every other man, may properly consider himself as one of the myriad agencies
through whom works the Unknown Cause; and
when the Unknown Cause produces in him a
certain belief he is thereby authorized to profess

and act out that belief." With this conclusion the limits of mental self-respect are transcended, and the theory breaks up in a melancholy farce. The theist may take some comfort, however, in remembering that his faith is no home-made fancy of his own, but a genuine product of the Unknown Cause, and he is thereby authorized to profess and act it out.

Two critical words in conclusion. First, it will be a distinct advance when we reach the insight that a theory is responsible for its implications and that the critical analysis of a theory is not an attack upon its holders. Secondly, it will be a still greater advance when the theory of knowledge is sufficiently developed to show that not every theory of things is compatible with the validity of knowledge. At present, in the uninstructed goodness of our hearts, we show the largest hospitality towards all theories without ever dreaming of inquiring into their bearings upon the problem of knowledge. If any critic points out that a given theory destroys reason and thus violates the conditions of all thinking, such is our good-nature that we conclude the consequences of the theory must be aberrations of the critic. The self-destructive